This is the first version of the **Civil PE Practice Exam and**

First Edition

Copyright © 2021 by Allison Franken

All rights reserved.

No part of this publication may be reproduced, distributed, or transmitted in any form or by any means, including photocopying, recording, or other electronic or mechanical methods without the prior written permission of the author.

Front cover image by Allison Franken.

Printed in the United States of America

First Printing September 2019

Allison Franken, P.E.
allyfranken@gmail.com

About the Author

I wrote this book shortly after taking the Civil: Water Resources and Environmental Professional Engineers Exam in April 2019. I graduated from Kansas State University in the spring of 2015 with a bachelor's degree in civil engineering. I started working at a large engineering firm in Kansas City, Missouri after graduation and have been there ever since.

I wanted to write this book to help fellow Civil PE test-takers get a feel of what the breadth exam is actually like. I hope you find this *Civil PE Practice Exam and Guide* useful and will use it as a study aid for the breadth portion of the Civil PE Exam.

    Allison Franken, P.E.
    allyfranken@gmail.com

Table of Contents   **Page No.**

1.0   WHAT IS THE PE EXAM 1
2.0   TESTING ELIGIBILITY 2
3.0   BREADTH EXAM MATERIAL 3
4.0   STUDY SCHEDULE 4
    4.1   CREATING YOUR STUDY SCHEDULE 4
5.0   EXAM DAY 7
    5.1   NCEES APPROVED CALCULATORS 7
    5.2   EXAM-ROOM RULES 7
    5.3   EXAM DAY FORMAT 8
    5.4   EXAM DAY CHECKLIST 9
6.0   EXAM RESULTS AND SCORING 10
7.0   HOW TO USE THIS BOOK 11
PRACTICE EXAM 12
ANSWER KEY: 40

Preface

I took the Civil: Water Resources and Environmental PE in April 2019 and had a wide range of study resources available to me. However, after a month of studying, I was frustrated with the prep material I was using. The practice tests seemed way too easy or way too difficult. Other options online seemed too expensive. That's exactly why I wanted to create this practice test.

The problems on this practice test are identical to the level of difficulty you will find on the actual exam. The solutions give detailed steps in solving the problems and you will never wonder where a number or equation came from.

I hope you find this practice exam helpful and advantageous in your studying.

1.0 WHAT IS THE PE EXAM

The Civil Professional Engineers Exam is an open-book, comprehensive civil engineering exam for licensure administered by NCEES – National Council of Examiners for Engineering and Surveying. The exam consists of a breadth and depth examination. This means that examinees work the breadth (AM) exam followed by one of the five depth (PM) exams. The five depth areas covered in the civil exam are construction, geotechnical, structural, transportation, and water resources and environmental. The breadth exam contains questions from all five areas of engineering. The depth exams focus on a single area of practice in civil engineering.

The exam is an 8-hour open book exam. The morning section contains 40 multiple-choice questions with a 4-hour time limit. The afternoon section contains 40 multiple-choice questions with a 4-hour time limit. Both International System of Units (SI) and US Customary System (USCS) units are used.

The exam contains both conceptual-type questions as well as design, analysis, and application type problems.

Civil PE Testing Services

2.0 TESTING ELIGIBILITY

Eligibility to sit for the PE exam varies by state or territory and is determined by each licensing board. State requirements can be found at https://ncees.org/state-links

Most states require four years of experience under a licensed Professional Engineer before sitting for the exam. However, a few states allow you take the test any time after passing the Fundamentals of Engineering (FE) Exam although you cannot apply for licensure until meeting the four-year experience requirement.

The test is offered twice a year, once in April and once in October. Some states only offer one testing location, while other states offer various locations.

The standard requirements for examination are:

(1) Taken and passed the NCEES Fundamental of Engineering (FE) Exam
(2) Have 4 years of satisfactory engineering experience (differs per state)
(3) Have an EAC ABET accredited degree in engineering or one deemed equivalent

Register for the Civil PE exam through your MyNCEES account at NCEES.org. Most licensing boards require PE examinees to file a state application and pay an application fee. In addition to the state application, most PE examinees will be required to pay actual test fees directly to NCEES during the registration process. You will receive a confirmation email from NCEES once you have successfully completed the registration process.

Civil PE Practice Exam and Guide

3.0 BREADTH EXAM MATERIAL

The civil engineering breadth exam consists of 40 multiple choice questions from the five areas of civil engineering: geotechnical, structural, water resources & environmental, transportation, and construction. The table below shows how many questions from each section will be on the exam:

Section	Number of Questions	Percentage of Test
Project Planning	4	10%
Means and Methods	3	7.5%
Soil Mechanics	6	15%
Structural Mechanics	6	15%
Hydraulics and Hydrology	7	17.5%
Geometrics	3	7.5%
Materials	6	15%
Site Development	5	5%
TOTAL:	**40**	**100%**

The specifications for the AM and PM exams can be found on the NCEES website.

4.0 STUDY SCHEDULE

The most important aspect for passing any discipline PE exam is to be and feel prepared on test day. The only way this can be accomplished is to practice, practice, practice. The test covers such a wide variety of topics that preparing can seem overwhelming. A great way to break up the studying is with a study schedule.

Ask yourself these questions before creating a study schedule:

1. How many days per week can I dedicate to studying?
2. What is my goal for hours to study per week?
3. What sections do I need to spend extra time on?
4. What could cause distraction in my study schedule?

It is recommended to dedicate at least 12 weeks to regular studying. Using these numbers as a guide, April tests takers should begin studying in January and October test takers should begin studying in July.

Remember, this 12-week studying period is for both breadth and depth content.

4.1 CREATING YOUR STUDY SCHEDULE

1. Set number of hours per week to study.

I would recommend studying at least 4 to 6 hours per day on the weekends and 1 to 2 hours three nights a week. You can break this up however you would like but try to aim for around 15 hours of studying per week to begin.

2. Take your hours per week times the total number of weeks.

(15 hours per week)(12 weeks) = 180 hours of studying. Divide this equally between breadth and depth content.

   90 hours for breadth content
   90 hours for depth content

3. Divide test sections into percent of the test.

There are 8 main topics covered on the breadth exam. Using the chart below, set the number of hours to study for each topic. The chart below uses 90 hours for breadth studying.

Section	Number of Questions	Percentage of Exam	Hours to Spend Studying
Project Planning	4	10%	9
Means and Methods	3	7.5%	6.75
Soil Mechanics	6	15%	13.5
Structural Mechanics	6	15%	13.5
Hydraulics and Hydrology	7	17.5%	15.75
Geometrics	3	7.5%	6.75
Materials	6	15%	13.5
Site Development	5	12.5%	11.25
TOTAL	**40**	**100%**	**90**

4. **Create a study schedule.**

An example study schedule is given on the next page. Use this as a guide when creating your own schedule.

Week Number	SUNDAY	MONDAY	TUESDAY	WEDNESDAY	THURSDAY	FRIDAY	SATURDAY
1	Project Planning		Project Planning		Project Planning		Means and Methods
2	Means and Methods		Soils		Soils		Soils
3	Soils			Structural	Structural		Structural
4	Structural		Geometrics	Geometrics			Materials
5	Materials			Site Development	Site Development		Site Development
6	Breadth Review		Breadth Review	Breadth Review	Breadth Review		Breadth Review
7	Depth			Depth			Depth
8	Depth		Depth		Depth		Depth
9	Depth			Depth			Depth
10	Depth		Depth		Depth		Depth
11	Depth			Depth			Depth
12	Depth Review		Depth Review	Depth Review	Depth Review		Depth Review

that Water Resources and Environmental is not included in the Breadth study section. It is not necessary clude your depth discipline in your breadth study schedule because you will cover it intensely in the depth dule.

Civil PE Practice Exam and Guide

5.0 EXAM DAY

The following sections provide a glimpse into the exam-day experience. Note that procedures may differ by location and state.

5.1 NCEES APPROVED CALCULATORS

To protect the integrity of its exams, NCEES limits the types of calculators examinees may bring to exam sites. The list of approved calculators is reviewed annually.

The following calculator models are the only ones acceptable for use during the 2018 and 2019 exams:

- **Casio:** All fx-115 and fx-991 models (Any Casio calculator must have "fx-115" or "fx-991" in its model name.)
- **Hewlett Packard:** The HP 33s and HP 35s models, but no others
- **Texas Instruments:** All TI-30X and TI-36X models (Any Texas Instruments calculator must have "TI-30X" or "TI-36X" in its model name.)

5.2 EXAM-ROOM RULES

You must agree to abide by the NCEES Candidate Agreement at all times. Examinees are required to sign their exam answer sheet before the exam starts to affirm that they have been provided the rules information, have read and understand the material, and agree to abide by the stated policies and procedures, which apply to all NCEES exams.

For exam admission, examinees must present their Exam Authorization and one of the following kinds of identification: (1) ID issued by a government entity in the country in which you are testing; (2) international travel passport in roman characters from your country of citizenship; or (3) U.S. military ID.

For the morning session, examinees must report to the exam site by the time shown on the Exam Authorization.

You are allowed to leave the room during the exam. To do so, you must take your test up to the proctor and pick it back up from them when you return.

Civil PE Practice Exam and Guide

5.3 EXAM DAY FORMAT

The schedule below gives a detailed outline of exam day.

TIME	ACTION
After Registering for Exam	Receive confirmation email from NCEES once you have successfully completed the registration process.
Two Weeks Before Exam Day	Receive email from NCEES with exam authorization. Your exam authorization will include a report time and location. • Exams are usually held in large hotel conference rooms • The room will consist of long tables all facing the front of the room. Two examinees will be assigned per table.

EXAM DAY

TIME	ACTION
7:15 AM	Exam report time, arrive at exam location.
7:15 - 7:45 AM	**Check in begins** for breadth exam. Depending on your exam location this can take some time. Try to be at the front of the line so you can get into the exam room and get settled. • Must show your Exam Authorization and ID • You will be given one mechanical pencil and ear plugs • Your seat is preassigned. Once in the room, find your seat and begin to set up and organize your reference material • Pack your reference material in something easily portable – wagons, suitcases, bins with wheels • Some locations make you take your reference material out of the crates or suitcases and place them along the back wall • Water is offered at the back of the room • DO NOT BRING YOUR CELL PHONE INTO THE EXAM ROOM
7:45 AM	Proctor hands out test booklets and reads instructions aloud. Sign your name agreeing to comply with NCEES rules.
8:00 AM – 12:00 PM	**Civil Breadth Exam**: 4-hour, 40 question breadth portion of exam. • 15-minute, 5-minute, and 1-minute warnings are given • If you finish the exam before the 15-minute warning, you can turn your test in and leave • If you finish the exam after the 15-minute warning, you must wait for the exam to end and for everyone to be dismissed

Civil PE Practice Exam and Guide

12:00 PM - 12:45 PM	**Lunch Break** • Exam materials cannot leave the exam room during the break • REMEMBER: take your exam authorization and ID with you to get back into the exam room post-lunch • Bring a lunch or plan on going somewhere quick – the 45 minutes goes by very quickly
12:45 PM	Check in for depth exam begins. Return to exam location at this time.
1:00 - 5:00 PM	**Civil Depth Exam:** 4-hour, 40 question depth portion of exam. • 15-minute, 5-minute, and 1-minute warnings are given • If you finish the exam before the 15-minute warning, you can turn your test in and leave • If you finish the exam after the 15-minute warning, you must wait for the exam to end and for everyone to be dismissed
5:00 PM	Exam dismissal

5.4   EXAM DAY CHECKLIST

To BRING

- **Exam authorization**
- **Form of identification**
- All reference materials
- NCEES approved calculator
- Snacks
- Plastic water bottle
- Ear plugs (you will be given one pair)
- Ruler or straight edge
- Car keys
- Lunch (leave in car)

TO LEAVE AT HOME:

- Scratch Paper (all work is done in the NCEES booklet)
- Cell Phone or other messaging devices
- Smart watches
- Pens, pencils, or erasers (you will be given an NCEES mechanical pencil)

6.0 EXAM RESULTS AND SCORING

Results for the Civil PE exam are generally released to the licensing boards 8-10 weeks after the exam administration. Depending on your state, you will be notified of your exam results online through your MyNCEES account or via postal mail from your state licensing board.

Exam results are reported pass/fail. NCEES provides a diagnostic report to all examinees who do not pass to help them identify the knowledge areas in which they need to improve before retaking the exam.

The pass rate for PE Civil examinations is generally around 60% depending on the depth discipline chosen.

7.0 HOW TO USE THIS BOOK

The solutions to the problems in this book are broken into three distinct steps:

STEP I – DEFINITIONS

It is important to know what the problem is about. For example, without knowing what "effective vertical stress" is on a geotechnical problem, it would be difficult to solve the problem. The definitions section of the solution quickly and simply describes the terms found in the problem and any terms that may be helpful to solve the problem.

The page number of the topic in the 16th edition of the CERM is also listed in this section – be sure to tab appropriately to what you think is necessary. The terms are listed in the following format:

TERM – CERM PAGE # - DEFINITION

STEP II – GAME PLAN

The most efficient way to solve a problem is to first take a broad approach. Before using any numbers or plugging and chugging, a game plan is given. The Game Plan lists what is given, what is being asked, and what steps will be taken to solve the problem.

STEP III – EXECUTE

Finally, the game plan is executed step by step. The solutions are easy to follow and show the quickest and easiest way to solve the problem. You will not wonder where a number came from or what steps were taken in the solution.

PRACTICE EXAM

This practice exam contains 40 multiple choice questions. Allow four hours to complete this practice exam. Utilize all reference material and only NCEES approved calculators. See Section 5.1 for a list of NCEES approved calculators. Do not use any computers or messaging devices.

Scantron® Sheet

Name _____ Date _____

Use this sheet to answer the multiple choice part of your test.

PLEASE NOTE
- Use only a no. 2 pencil.
- Example: Ⓐ ● Ⓒ Ⓓ
- Erase changes COMPLETELY.

Mark one answer for each question.

1. Ⓐ Ⓑ Ⓒ Ⓓ
2. Ⓐ Ⓑ Ⓒ Ⓓ
3. Ⓐ Ⓑ Ⓒ Ⓓ
4. Ⓐ Ⓑ Ⓒ Ⓓ
5. Ⓐ Ⓑ Ⓒ Ⓓ
6. Ⓐ Ⓑ Ⓒ Ⓓ
7. Ⓐ Ⓑ Ⓒ Ⓓ
8. Ⓐ Ⓑ Ⓒ Ⓓ
9. Ⓐ Ⓑ Ⓒ Ⓓ
10. Ⓐ Ⓑ Ⓒ Ⓓ
11. Ⓐ Ⓑ Ⓒ Ⓓ
12. Ⓐ Ⓑ Ⓒ Ⓓ
13. Ⓐ Ⓑ Ⓒ Ⓓ
14. Ⓐ Ⓑ Ⓒ Ⓓ
15. Ⓐ Ⓑ Ⓒ Ⓓ
16. Ⓐ Ⓑ Ⓒ Ⓓ
17. Ⓐ Ⓑ Ⓒ Ⓓ
18. Ⓐ Ⓑ Ⓒ Ⓓ
19. Ⓐ Ⓑ Ⓒ Ⓓ
20. Ⓐ Ⓑ Ⓒ Ⓓ
21. Ⓐ Ⓑ Ⓒ Ⓓ
22. Ⓐ Ⓑ Ⓒ Ⓓ
23. Ⓐ Ⓑ Ⓒ Ⓓ
24. Ⓐ Ⓑ Ⓒ Ⓓ
25. Ⓐ Ⓑ Ⓒ Ⓓ
26. Ⓐ Ⓑ Ⓒ Ⓓ
27. Ⓐ Ⓑ Ⓒ Ⓓ
28. Ⓐ Ⓑ Ⓒ Ⓓ
29. Ⓐ Ⓑ Ⓒ Ⓓ
30. Ⓐ Ⓑ Ⓒ Ⓓ
31. Ⓐ Ⓑ Ⓒ Ⓓ
32. Ⓐ Ⓑ Ⓒ Ⓓ
33. Ⓐ Ⓑ Ⓒ Ⓓ
34. Ⓐ Ⓑ Ⓒ Ⓓ
35. Ⓐ Ⓑ Ⓒ Ⓓ
36. Ⓐ Ⓑ Ⓒ Ⓓ
37. Ⓐ Ⓑ Ⓒ Ⓓ
38. Ⓐ Ⓑ Ⓒ Ⓓ
39. Ⓐ Ⓑ Ⓒ Ⓓ
40. Ⓐ Ⓑ Ⓒ Ⓓ

Problem 1

A single dump truck with a capacity of 15 cubic yards hauls excavated material from a project site. An excavator with a bucket capacity of 5 cubic yards loads the excavated material into the dump truck. Loading time for each bucket is 45 seconds. The distance to the dump site is 6 miles and the average speed of the dump truck is 35 miles per hour. Dumping time is 30 seconds. A workday is 8 hours. How many days will it take to excavate and haul 20,000 cubic yards of material?

A) 36
B) 65
C) 108
D) 193

Problem 2

A city needs to expand their wastewater treatment plant to allow for future population growth. The city is trying to decide between the two options in the table below. Given an annual interest rate of 4% and a lifespan of 30 years, determine which option's present worth is more cost effective.

Item	Option I	Option II
Initial Cost	$1,300,000	$1,500,000
Annual Maintenance	$50,000	$20,000
Salvage Value	$200,000	$140,000

A) Option I
B) Option II
C) The options cost the same
D) Not enough information

Problem 3

A projected project schedule is given below. Assume even workload distribution per task. As of July 1, what percent of the project is complete and is the project ahead or behind schedule?

Task	% of Project	J	F	M	A	M	J	J	A	S	O	N	D	% Complete as of July 1
		PROJECTED SCHEDULE - MONTH												
Civil	20%													100%
Electrical	40%													80%
Mechanical	10%													60%
Structural	30%													10%

A) 39%, ahead of schedule
B) 39%, behind schedule
C) 61%, ahead of schedule
D) 61%, behind schedule

Problem 4

Using the project schedule below, determine the float (days) for Activity D.

A) 0
B) 2
C) 4
D) 5

Activity	Duration (Days)	Predecessor
A	4	-
B	8	A
C	6	A
D	3	B
E	7	C
F	3	C
G	2	E, F
H	2	D, G

Problem 5

Which of the following joints is used when concrete has been poured at different times?

A) Contraction Joint
B) Isolation Joint
C) Control Joint
D) Construction Joint

Problem 6

A 20-foot wall form subjected to a 10 psf wind load is shown in the figure below. Diagonal braces 8-foot on center along the length of the wall prevent the brace from overturning. What is the axial force (lb/ft) resisted by the brace per unit width of wall?

A) 81
B) 202
C) 1143
D) 1616

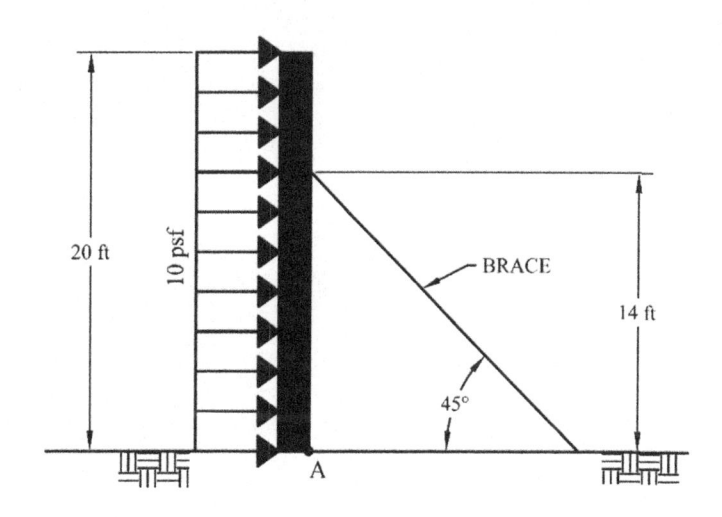

Problem 7

For the cable system shown, the tension (kips) in cable AB is most nearly:

A) 42.4
B) 44.6
C) 56.5
D) 58.0

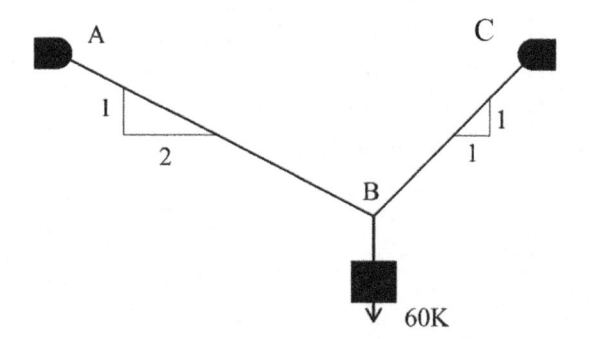

Problem 8

A 10-ft tall concrete gravity retaining wall having a unit weight of 150 pcf is shown in the figure. The Rankine active earth pressure (lb/ft) is most nearly:

A) 536
B) 2300
C) 2437
D) 2719

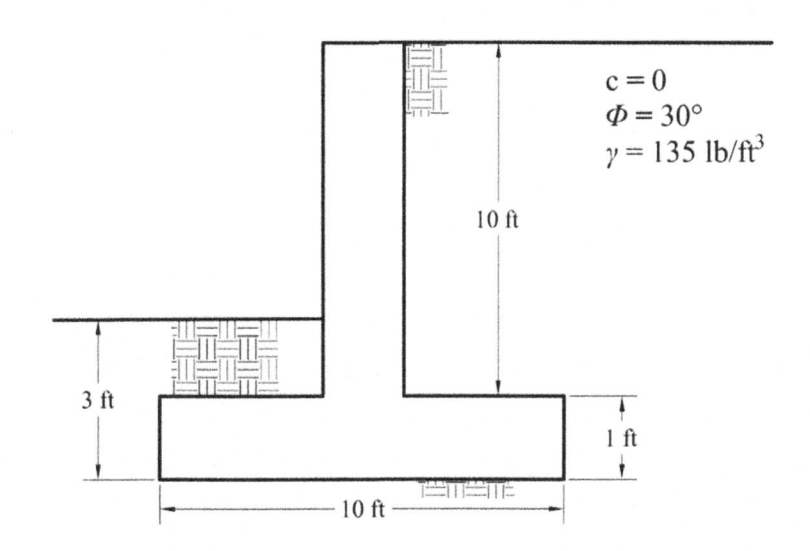

$c = 0$
$\Phi = 30°$
$\gamma = 135 \text{ lb/ft}^3$

10 ft
3 ft
1 ft
10 ft

Problem 9

A 5'x 5' footing is to be constructed near an existing 24" stormsewer. What increase in pressure, in psf, will the center of the pipe experience due to the construction of the footing?

A) 20
B) 34
C) 35
D) 500

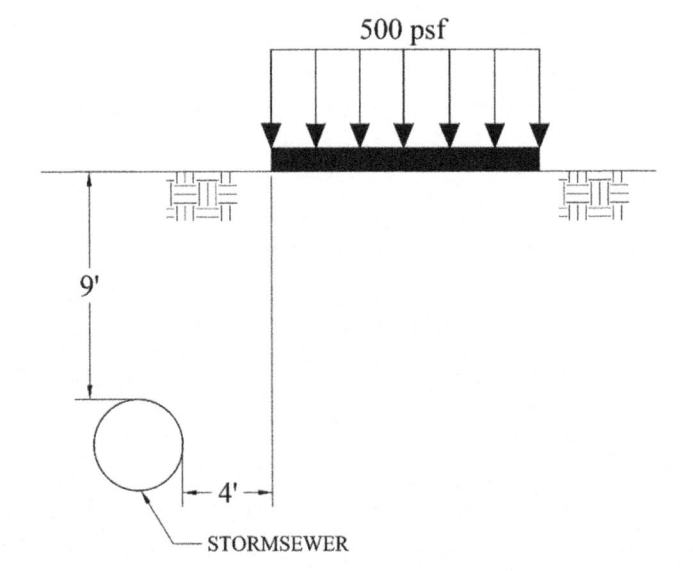

Problem 10

Which statement is most true about point B when the water table is raised from point B to point A?

A) The effective stress and pore pressure increase
B) The effective stress and pore pressure decrease
C) The effective stress increases and pore pressure decreases
D) The effective stress decreases and pore pressure increases

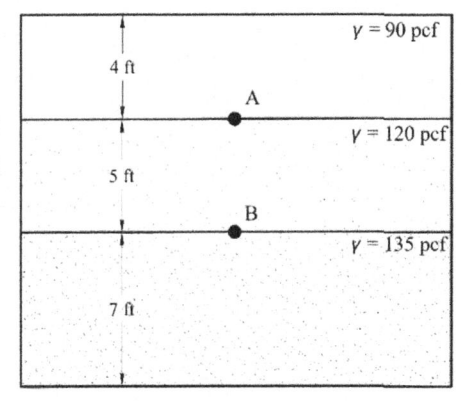

Problem 11

A uniformly distributed surface load is applied to the ground surface. The primary consolidation, in inches, for the normally consolidated clay shown below is:

A) 0.9
B) 1.2
C) 1.8
D) 2.6

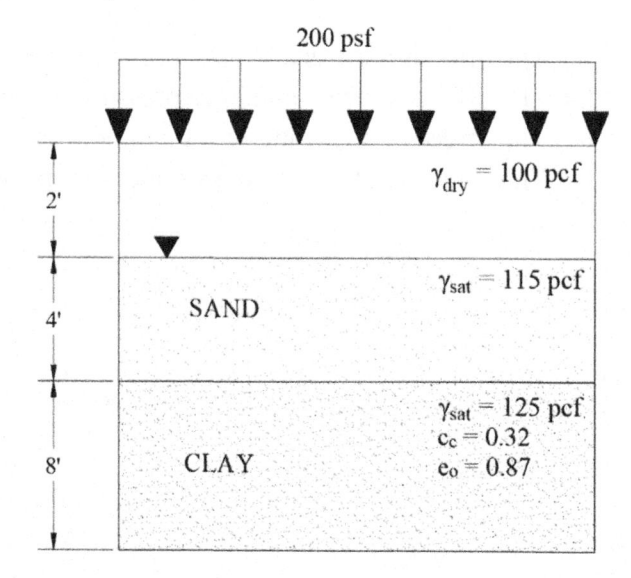

Load: 200 psf

- 2' $\gamma_{dry} = 100$ pcf
- 4' SAND, $\gamma_{sat} = 115$ pcf
- 8' CLAY, $\gamma_{sat} = 125$ pcf, $c_c = 0.32$, $e_o = 0.87$

Problem 12

An earthen dam is initially dry. If the water table is rapidly raised to the level shown, the dam's factor of safety against slope failure will:

A) Increase
B) Decrease
C) Stay the same
D) Not enough information

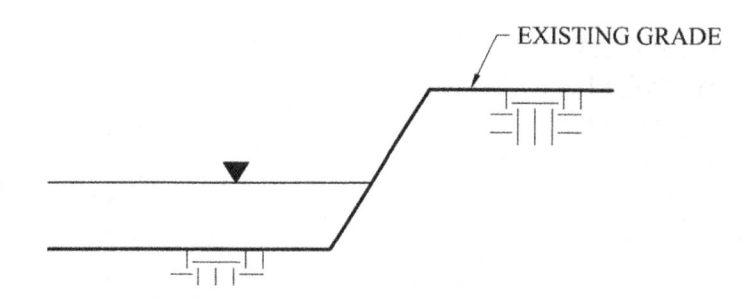

Problem 13

A 4' x 4' square footing is shown below. The factor of safety is 3.0. The maximum net allowable bearing capacity, in psf, is:

A) 11,996
B) 13,559
C) 13,689
D) 15,074

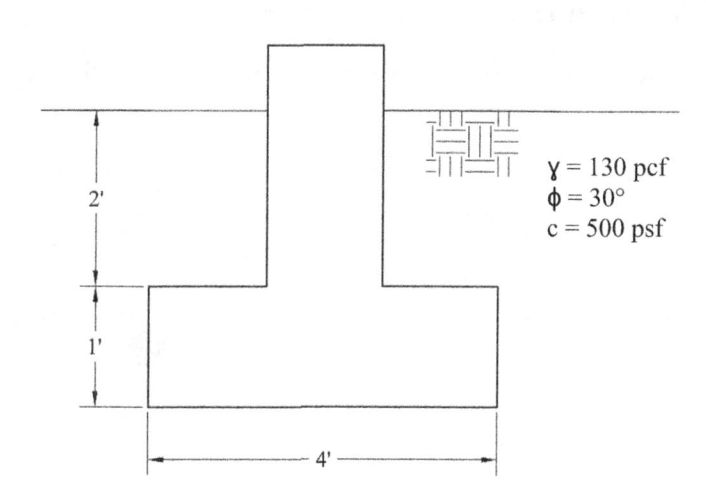

γ = 130 pcf
ϕ = 30°
c = 500 psf

Problem 14

The stress-strain curve for a steel beam is shown below. The maximum tensile strength occurs at which point?

A) Point A
B) Point B
C) Point C
D) Point D

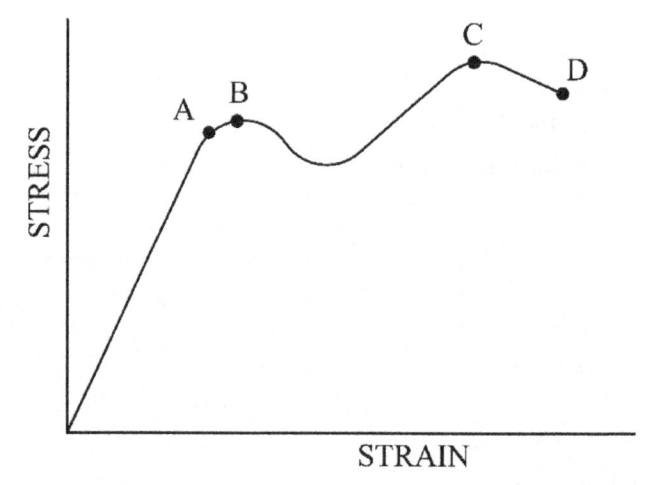

Problem 15

The beam shown below has one pin and one roller connection. The maximum shear force, in kips, in the beam is:

A) 4.2
B) 12.0
C) 13.6
D) 20.0

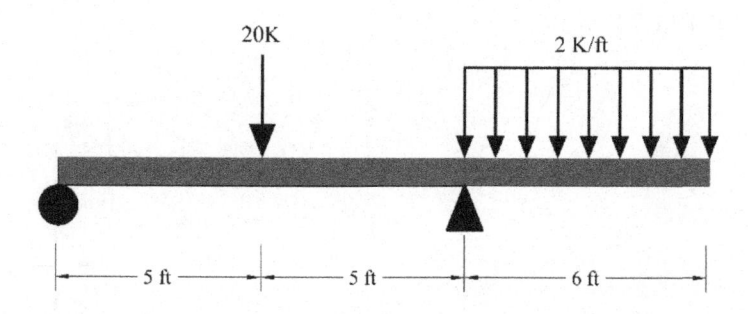

Problem 16

Analyze the truss shown. The force in member BE, in kips, is most nearly:

A) 1.6
B) 3.7
C) 4.2
D) 5.8

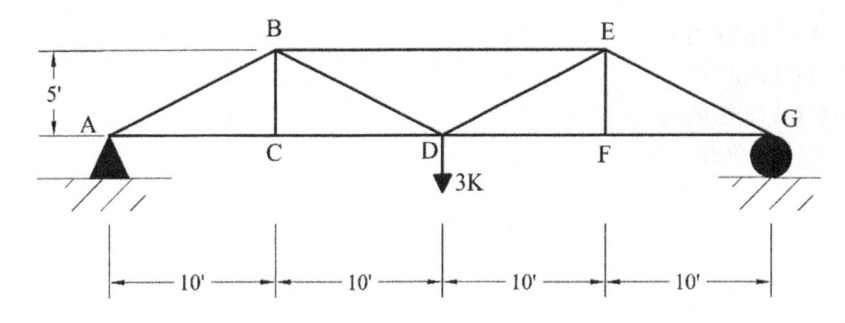

Problem 17

The elongation, in inches, of the 1-foot diameter cylinder due to the applied load is most nearly:

A) 0.000763
B) 0.0000212
C) 0.0000636
D) 0.00000176

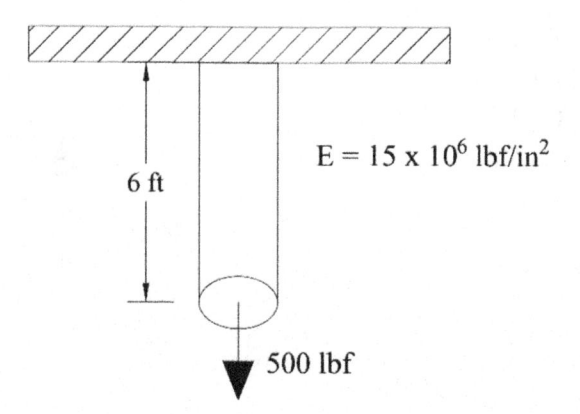

$E = 15 \times 10^6 \text{ lbf/in}^2$

6 ft

500 lbf

Problem 18

The T beam below experiences a bending moment of 1.4 k-ft. The max bending stress in the beam, in psi, is most nearly:

A) 117
B) 125
C) 473
D) 545

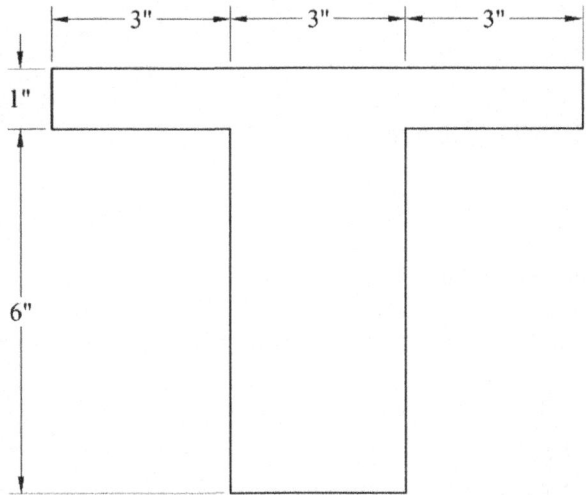

Problem 19

The design criteria for all sections in a structural beam are:

A) $\varphi M_n \geq M_u$
B) $\varphi M_n \geq V_u$
C) $V_u \geq \varphi V_n$
D) All the above

Problem 20

The head loss, in feet, through Branch B is most nearly:

A) 4.2
B) 6.8
C) 8.0
D) 14.0

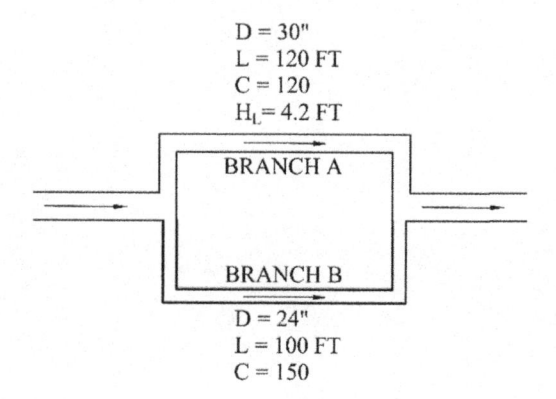

BRANCH A
D = 30"
L = 120 FT
C = 120
H_L = 4.2 FT

BRANCH B
D = 24"
L = 100 FT
C = 150

Problem 21

A 48-inch concrete pipe (n = 0.013) flows full during a 100-year rain event. The pipe collects runoff from a 5-acre area. The slope of the pipe is 2%. What is the flow rate, in cfs, under full conditions?

A) 128
B) 204
C) 13,000
D) 154,000

Problem 22

Rain falls onto three subcatchments as described in the table below. Rainfall intensity is 4.0 inches per hour. The peak runoff, in cfs, for the three watersheds is most nearly:

A) 5.6
B) 8.3
C) 12.0
D) 26.0

Subcatchment	Area (acre)	Lag (min)	C
I	3.2	20	0.65
II	2.0	48	0.70
III	4.2	55	0.72

Problem 23

The profile of an open channel is shown below. The hydraulic radius of section C, in feet, is most nearly:

A) 2.0
B) 3.6
C) 4.7
D) 6.5

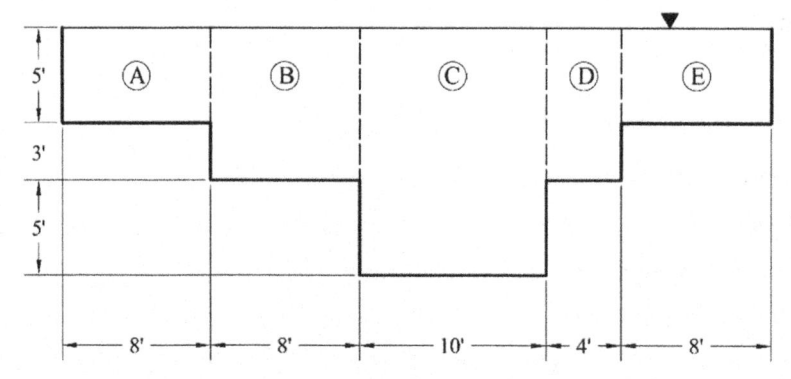

Problem 24

Which flow measurement device is used in pressure pipes?

A) Triangular Weir
B) Parshall Flume
C) Orifice Meter
D) Spillway

Problem 25

A 4-hour storm produces a produces a total runoff of 50 acre-ft for a 120-acre watershed. The peak discharge is 650 cfs. The peak discharge for a 4-hour storm producing 3-inches of net precipitation is most nearly:

A) 121
B) 390
C) 650
D) 741

Problem 26

An 8-inch diameter pipe under 100 psi of pressure discharges through a 2-inch diameter nozzle. Assuming a nozzle coefficient of 1.0, the flow rate through the nozzle, in cfs, is most nearly:

A) 2.65
B) 9.41
C) 42.5
D) 80.2

Problem 27

A 1600-foot-long sag vertical curve joins a tangent of -4% to a tangent of 3%. The BVC is located at stationing 25+00 and elevation 171.00 ft. The elevation and stationing of the lowest point on the curve are most nearly:

	Elevation (ft)	Stationing (ft)
A)	152.7 ft	34+14
B)	152.7 ft	31+85
C)	189.3 ft	34+14
D)	189.3 ft	31+85

Problem 28

A circular horizontal curve with length of 2000 feet is shown below. The middle ordinate, measured in feet, is most nearly:

A) 145
B) 150
C) 155
D) 160

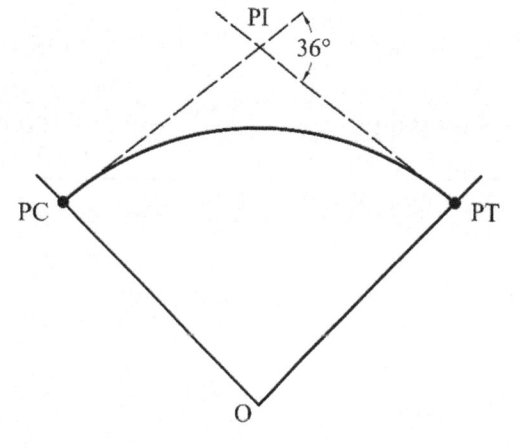

Problem 29

Given the following information, determine the annual number of buses in the design lane for a two-lane highway.

AADT = 6000	LOS = C
Peak Factor = 2.0	% Cars = 50%
FFS = 60 mph	% Trucks = 30%
No. lanes each direction = 1	% Buses = 20%
Directional Design = 60/40	

A) 480
B) 720
C) 262,800
D) 438,000

Problem 30

What is the best way to compact clean gravel?

A) Vibratory Roller Compactor
B) Pneumatic Rubber Tire Roller
C) Sheepsfoot Roller Compactor
D) Smooth-wheel Roller

Problem 31

The strength over time graph for Portland Cement Type I is shown below. The strength over time graph for Portland Cement Type III is most nearly:

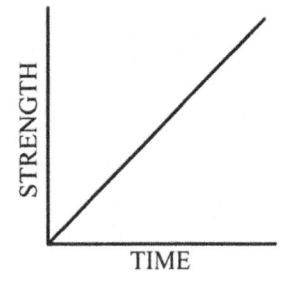

Portland Cement Type I

A)

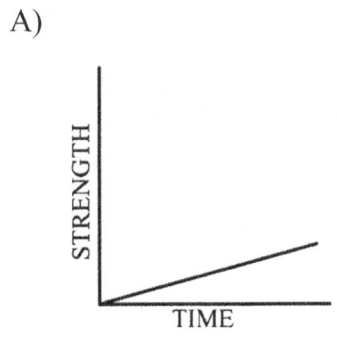

B)

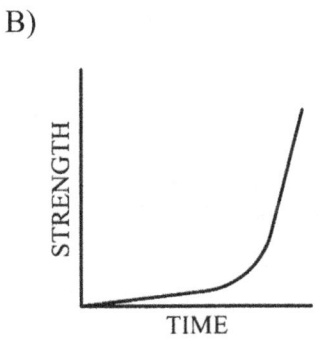

C)

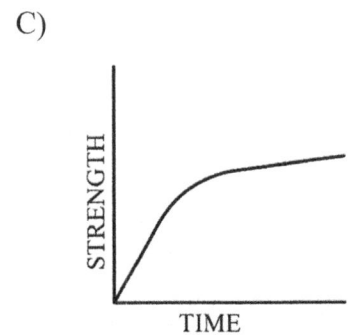

D)

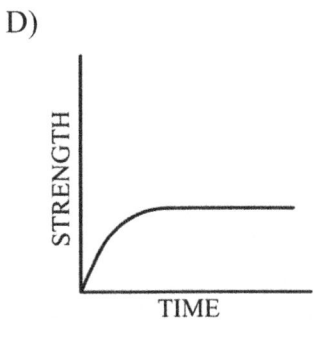

Problem 32

A soil is under investigation. Mechanical and Plasticity limits are shown below. According to the Unified Soil Classification System (USCS), the soil may be classified as:

| Mechanical Analysis || Plasticity ||
Sieve	% Finer	Liquid Limit	Plastic Limit
10	85%	62	26
40	70%		
200	61%		

A) Fat Clay
B) Lean Clay
C) MH
D) LH

Problem 33

A soil sample has a specific gravity of 2.65. What is the dry unit weight (lb/ft^3) if the soil's water content is 16% and degree of saturation is 73%?

A) 105
B) 107
C) 111
D) 112

Problem 34

A new construction project requires 200,000 cubic feet of fill. The soil used for fill is to be excavated and hauled from a nearby borrow pit. The borrow soil has a shrinkage factor of 14% and a swell factor of 11%. The required soil volume in cubic yards to be hauled from the borrow pit is most nearly:

A) 9,490
B) 9,560
C) 256,200
D) 258,140

Problem 35

The results of 28-day concrete cylinder breaks are shown below. The concrete molds are 4" x 8". The 28-day compressive strength, in psi, is most nearly:

A) 10
B) 2437
C) 2666
D) 9753

Cylinder No.	Failure Loading (Kips)
1	130
2	128
3	114
4	118

Problem 36

The side of a hill is to be excavated for construction of a new 60 ft x 60 ft building. The length of excavation will be 200 ft. How many cubic yards of material will need to be excavated?

A) 1,335
B) 4,445
C) 36,000
D) 120,000

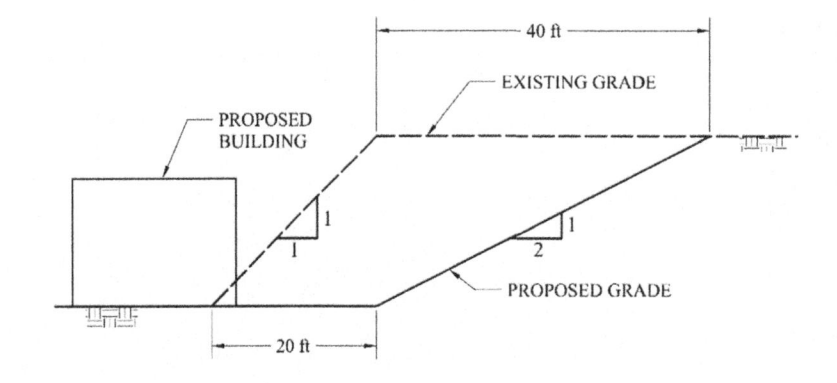

Problem 37

Two wells exist at points A and B. A new well is to be constructed at point C. The coordinates of the points are shown in the figure below. The bearing of line AC is most nearly:

A) N31°E
B) N59°E
C) N31°W
D) S59°W

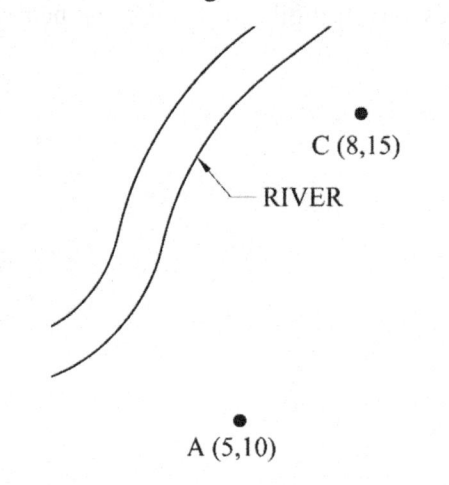

Problem 38

The erosion and sediment control feature best used to reduce runoff flow rate is:

A) Silt Fence
B) Sediment Structure
C) Erosion Control Fabric
D) Check Dam

Problem 39

The profile and mass diagrams for a construction project are shown below. Which statement is true?

A) Section B-C represents a fill operation
B) The job transitions from cut to fill at station C
C) The net cut/fill is zero
D) B and C

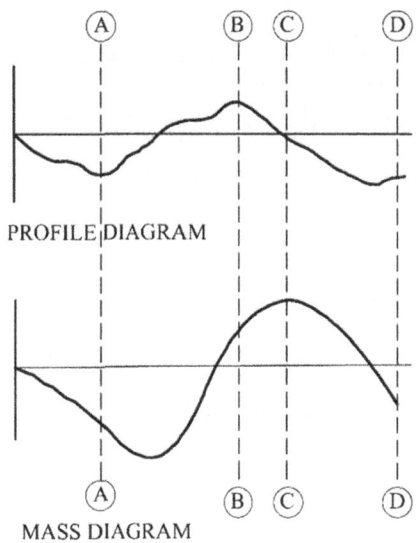

Problem 40

OSHA requires that fall protection be provided for each employee walking or working on an elevated surface. This regulation applies to elevated surfaces, measured in feet, that exceed a height of:

A) 4
B) 6
C) 10
D) 12

ANSWER KEY:

1	B		21	B
2	B		22	D
3	D		23	D
4	C		24	C
5	D		25	B
6	B		26	A
7	B		27	A
8	D		28	C
9	A		29	C
10	D		30	A
11	C		31	C
12	A		32	A
13	A		33	A
14	C		34	B
15	C		35	D
16	D		36	B
17	B		37	A
18	D		38	D
19	A		39	B
20	A		40	B

Problem 1 Solution

A single dump truck with a capacity of 15 cubic yards hauls excavated material from a project site. An excavator with a bucket capacity of 5 cubic yards loads the excavated material into the dump truck. Loading time for each bucket is 45 seconds. The distance to the dump site is 6 miles and the average speed of the dump truck is 35 miles per hour. Dumping time is 30 seconds. A workday is 8 hours. How many days will it take to excavate and haul 20,000 cubic yards of material?

A) 36
B) 65
C) 108
D) 193

SOLUTION

I. DEFINITIONS

No definitions required to complete this problem.

II. GAME PLAN

1. Calculate the total time for one round trip.
   - **1a.** Calculate loading time.
   - **1b.** Calculate round trip drive time.
   - **1c.** Calculate dumping time.
2. Calculate number of trips required.

III. EXECUTE

1. Calculate the total time for one round trip.
   - **1a.** Calculate loading time.

$$\frac{\text{dump truck capacity}}{\text{bucket capacity}} = \text{buckets per truck}$$

$$\frac{15 \frac{yd^3}{truck}}{5 \frac{yd^3}{truck}} = 3 \frac{\text{buckets}}{\text{truck}}$$

Load time per bucket = 45 seconds

$$\left(3 \frac{\text{buckets}}{\text{truck}}\right)\left(45 \frac{\text{seconds}}{\text{bucket}}\right) = 135 \frac{\text{seconds}}{\text{truck}}$$

$$\left(135 \frac{\text{seconds}}{\text{truck}}\right)\left(\frac{1 \text{ min}}{60 \text{ seconds}}\right) = \mathbf{2.25 \text{ minutes loading time}}$$

1b. Calculate round trip drive time.

(distance one way)(2) = roundtrip distance

(6 miles)(2) = 12 miles roundtrip

$$\frac{12 \text{ miles}}{35 \frac{\text{miles}}{\text{hour}}} = 0.34 \text{ hours}$$

$$(0.34 \text{ hour})\left(\frac{60 \text{ minutes}}{1 \text{ hour}}\right) = \mathbf{20.57 \text{ minutes roundtrip drive time}}$$

1c. Calculate dumping time.

Dumping time is given = 30 seconds = **0.5 minutes dumping time**

Sum steps 1a through 1c to get total round-trip time.

2.25 min + 20.57 min + 0.5 min = 23.32 minutes for one round trip

2. Calculate number of trips required.

$$\frac{\text{volume of excavation required}}{\text{capacity of truck}} = \text{loads required}$$

$$\left(\frac{20{,}000 \text{ yd}^3}{15 \text{ yd}^3}\right) = 1334 \text{ loads required}$$

(loads required)(round trip time) = total time required

$$(1334 \text{ loads})\left(23.32 \frac{\text{min}}{\text{load}}\right) = 31{,}109 \text{ min} = 519 \text{ hours required}$$

$$\frac{\text{total time required}}{\text{hours per workday}} = \text{total days required}$$

$$\left(\frac{519 \text{ hours}}{8 \frac{\text{hours}}{\text{day}}}\right) = 64.89 \text{ days} = \mathbf{65 \text{ days}}$$

THE CORRECT ANSWER IS B.

Problem 2 Solution

A city needs to expand their wastewater treatment plant to allow for future population growth. The city is trying to decide between the two options in the table below. Given an annual interest rate of 4% and a lifespan of 30 years, determine which option's present worth is more cost effective.

Item	Option I	Option II
Initial Cost	$1,300,000	$1,500,000
Annual Maintenance	$50,000	$20,000
Salvage Value	$200,000	$140,000

A) Option I
B) Option II
C) The options cost the same
D) Not enough information

SOLUTION

I. DEFINITIONS

- Cash Flow Diagram – **CERM 87-3** – A diagram drawn to help visualize and simplify problems having diverse receipts and disbursements
- Single Payment Cash Flow – **CERM 87-4** – A single amount paid or received all at one time
- Uniform Series Cash Flow – **CERM 87-4** – A payment consisting of equal transactions starting at t = 1 and ending at t = n
- Present Worth (P) – **CERM 87-6** – The equivalence of any future amount, F, at time t = n to any present amount
- Future Worth (F) – **CERM 87-5** – The equivalence of any present amount, P, at time t = 0 to any future amount
- Interest Rate (i) – **CERM 87-5** – The proportion of a loan that is charged as interest to the borrower per period
- Salvage Value – **CERM 87-19** – The estimated resale value of an asset at the end of its useful life

II. GAME PLAN

1. Draw the Cash Flow Diagram for each option.
2. Calculate the present worth of the Initial Costs.
3. Calculate the present worth of the Annual Maintenances.
   3a. Calculate the A to P factor.
   3b. Apply factor to Annual Maintenances.
4. Calculate the present worth of the Salvage Values.
5. Sum present worths.

6. Compare options I and II.

III. EXECUTE

1. Draw the Cash Flow Diagram for each option.

   Option I.

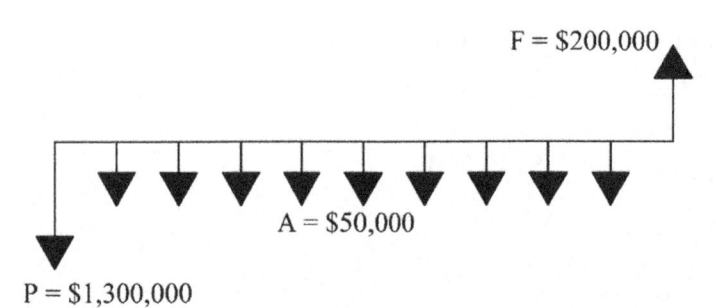

   F = $200,000

   A = $50,000

   P = $1,300,000

   Option II.

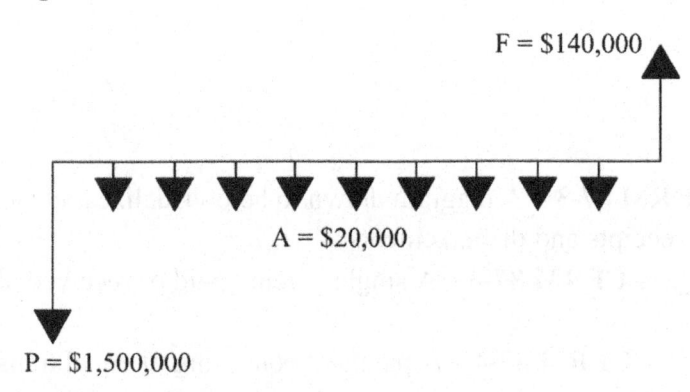

   F = $140,000

   A = $20,000

   P = $1,500,000

2. Calculate the present worth of the Initial Costs.

   The initial costs are already in present worth; therefore no calculation is necessary.

   Option I.

   P = $1,300,000

   Option II.

   P = $1,500,000

3. Calculate the present worth of the Annual Maintenances.

   3a. Calculate the A to P factor

   The A to P factor is the conversion factor to find P given A. The factor is multiplied by the A value to determine P.

   $$\frac{P}{A} = \frac{(1+i)^n - 1}{i(1+i)^n}$$ **CERM Table 87.1 (A to P)**

   Where:

i = interest rate, %

n = number of periods

P = present worth

A = uniform series amount

$$\frac{P}{A} = \frac{(1+0.04)^{30}-1}{0.04(1+0.04)^{30}}$$

$$\frac{P}{A} = \mathbf{17.29}$$

3b. Apply factor to Annual Maintenances.

Option I.

$P = 17.29(\text{Annual Maintenance})$

$P = 17.29(\$50,000)$

$\mathbf{P = \$864,500}$

Option II.

$P = 17.29(\text{Annual Maintenance})$

$P = 17.29(\$20,000)$

$\mathbf{P = \$345,800}$

4. Calculate the present worth of the Salvage Values.

$P = F(1+i)^{-n}$ **CERM EQ 87.3**

Option I.

$P = F(1+i)^{-n}$

$P = \$200,000(1+0.04)^{-30}$

$\mathbf{P = \$61,664}$

Option II.

$P = F(1+i)^{-n}$

$P = \$140,000(1+0.04)^{-30}$

$\mathbf{P = \$43,165}$

5. Sum present worths.

Present Worth = Initial Cost + Present Annual Maintenance − Present Salvage

	Option I	Option II
Initial Cost	$1,300,000	$1,500,000
Present Annual Maintenance	$864,500	$345,800
Present Salvage Value	$61,664	$43,165
Total Cost	**$2,102,836**	**$1,802,635**

6. Compare options I and II.

   Option I = 2.1 million

   Option II = $1.8 million

   Option II is more cost effective.

THE CORRECT ANSWER IS B.

Problem 3 Solution

A projected project schedule is given below. Assume even workload distribution per task. As of July 1, what percent of the project is complete and is the project ahead or behind schedule?

		\multicolumn{12}{c}{PROJECTED SCHEDULE - MONTH}	
Task	% of Project	J	F	M	A	M	J	J	A	S	O	N	D	% Complete as of July 1
Civil	20%													100%
Electrical	40%													80%
Mechanical	10%													60%
Structural	30%													10%

A) 39%, ahead of schedule
B) 39%, behind schedule
C) 61%, ahead of schedule
D) 61%, behind schedule

SOLUTION

I. DEFINITIONS

- Gantt Chart – **CERM 86-10** – A horizontal bar chart used to graphically schedule and monitor projects

II. GAME PLAN

1. Calculate actual percent project completion by using weighted average.
2. Calculate planned percent project completion by using weighted average.
3. Compare actual versus planned.

III. EXECUTE

1. Calculate actual percent project completion by using weighted average.

    Actual Completion is the percentage of the task that is <u>actually complete</u> as of July 1. This is given in the "% Complete as of July 1" column in the projected schedule.

    Actual Project Completion = $100\% \sum (\%\text{ of Project})(\%\text{ Complete as of July 1})$

    Actual Completion = $100\%[(0.20)(1.00) + (0.40)(0.80) + (0.10)(0.60) + (0.30)(0.10)]$

    Actual Completion = 61%

2. Calculate planned percent project completion by using weighted average.

Planned Completion is the percentage of the task that should be completed by July 1. This is found by counting the boxes in the Gantt Chart. For example, the Mechanical task spans 6 squares (April-September). According to the Gantt Chart, as of July 1 50% (3 out of 6 boxes) of the Mechanical task is planned completed, however 60% is actually completed.

Planned Completion = 100% Σ(% of Project)(% Planned Completion)

Planned Completion = 100%[(0.20)(1.00) + (0.40)(1.00) + (0.10)(0.50) + (0.30)(0.25)]

Planned Completion = 72.5%

3. Compare actual versus planned.

   Actual Completion = 61%

   Planed Comletion = 72.5%

   Actual < Plan, therefore the project is behind schedule.

THE CORRECT ANSWER IS D.

Problem 4 Solution

Using the project schedule below, determine the float (days) for Activity D.

A) 0
B) 2
C) 4
D) 5

Activity	Duration (Days)	Predecessor
A	4	-
B	8	A
C	6	A
D	3	B
E	7	C
F	3	C
G	2	E, F
H	2	D, G

SOLUTION

I. DEFINITIONS

- Activity on Node Network – **CERM 86-11** - A precedence diagram method which uses boxes to denote schedule activities
- Critical Path Method (CPM) – **CERM 86-11** - A directed graph that describes the precedence of project activities
- Early Start (ES) – **CERM 86-11** - Earliest possible start date for an activity
- Late Start (LS) – **CERM 86-11** - Latest possible start date for an activity
- Early Finish (EF) – **CERM 86-11** - Earliest possible finish date for an activity
- Late Finish (LF) – **CERM 86-11** - Latest possible finish date for an activity
- Float – **CERM 86-12** - The amount of time an activity can be delayed without affecting the overall project schedule
- Critical Path – **CERM 86-12** - Sequence of activities that must all be started and finished exactly on time in order to not delay the project

II. GAME PLAN

1. Draw the Activity on Node Network.
2. Determine Early Start (ES) and Early Finish (EF) for all activities.
3. Determine Critical Path.
4. Determine EF/LF for activity D.
5. Determine float for activity D.

III. EXECUTE

1. Draw the Activity on Node Network.

   Fill in the Activity (ACT) and Duration (DUR) boxes using the template below.

ES	ACT	EF
LS	DUR	LF

Civil PE Practice Exam and Guide

Activity — A 4 — Duration

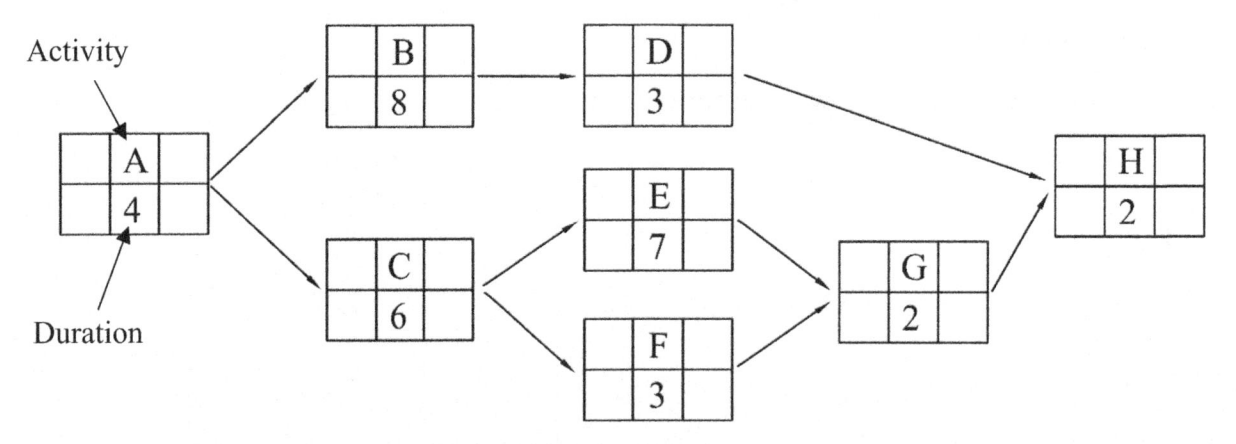

[Network diagram: A(4) → B(8) → D(3) → H(2); A(4) → C(6) → E(7) → G(2) → H(2); C(6) → F(3) → G(2)]

2. Determine Early Start (ES) and Early Finish (EF) for all activities.

   2a. Start with Activity A and beginning at Day 0 and work toward Activity H.

   Early Start + Duration = Early Finish

   2b. Early Start for activity A is 0. Duration is 4 days.

   Early Finish = 0 + 4 = 4 days

   2c. Move onto Activity B. ES for Activity B is the EF for Activity A.

   ES = 4, Dur = 8, therefore EF = 4 + 8 = 12

   2d. Complete this for the remainder of the activities.

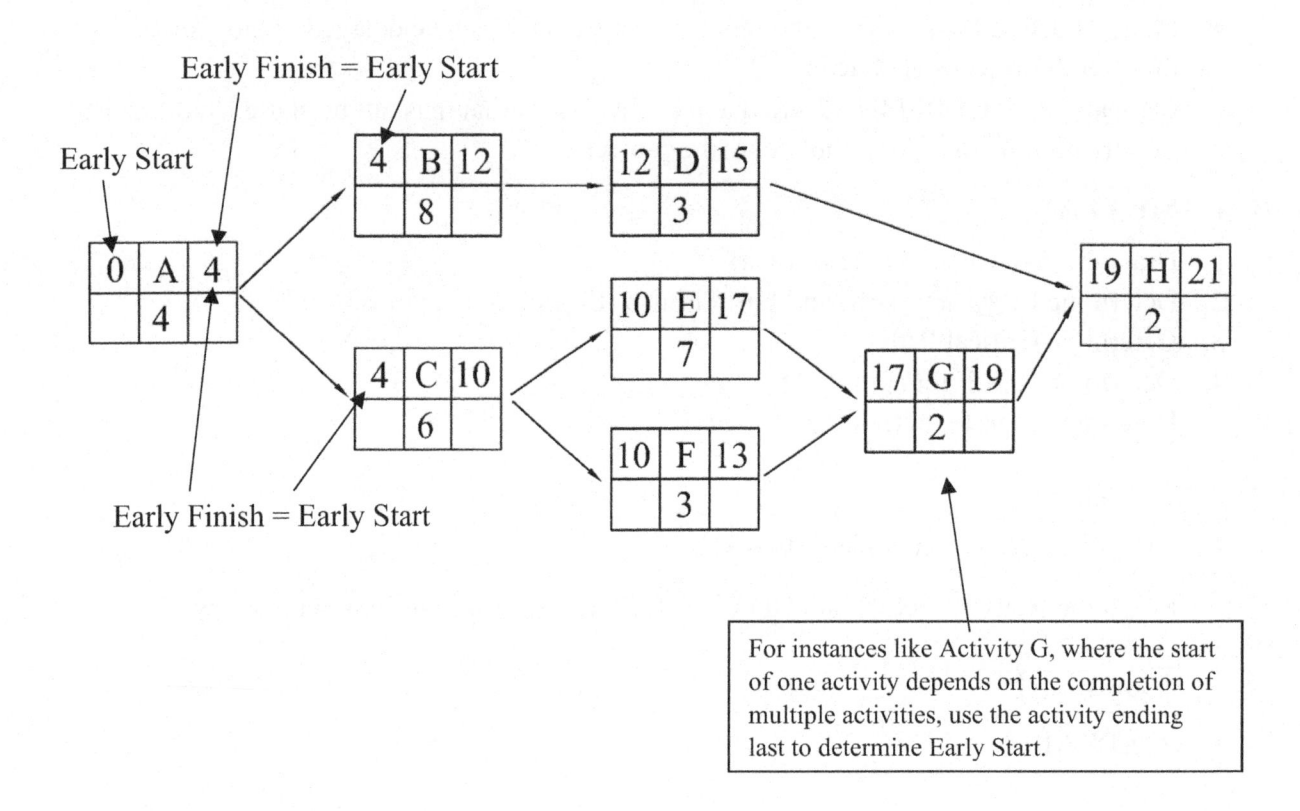

[Network diagram with Early Start/Early Finish values:
- 0 | A | 4, duration 4
- 4 | B | 12, duration 8
- 12 | D | 15, duration 3
- 4 | C | 10, duration 6
- 10 | E | 17, duration 7
- 10 | F | 13, duration 3
- 17 | G | 19, duration 2
- 19 | H | 21, duration 2]

Early Finish = Early Start
Early Start
Early Finish = Early Start

For instances like Activity G, where the start of one activity depends on the completion of multiple activities, use the activity ending last to determine Early Start.

Civil PE Testing Services

3. Determine Critical Path.

   3a. Work backwards from Activity H. The Float (LS – ES or LF – EF) is zero along the critical path.

   3b. EF for activity H is 21, therefore LF must also be 21 to keep the project from being delayed. Duration of Activity H is 2 days, 21 – 2 = 19. The latest Activity H can start without delaying the project is Day 19.

   3c. Work backwards to Activity A using the same process.

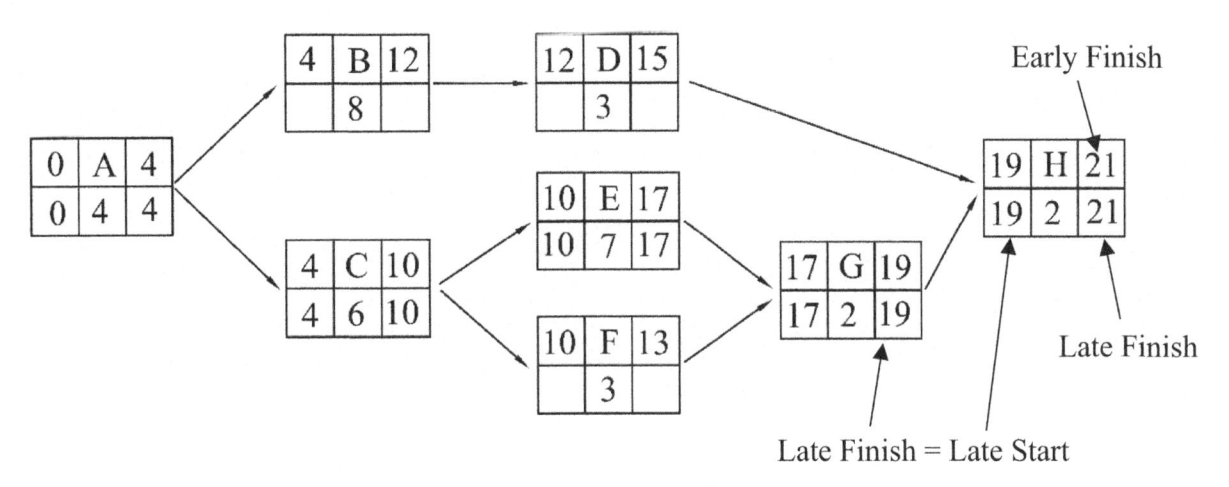

4. Determine LS/LF for Activity D.

   4a. Activity D is not part of the critical path. Therefore, Activity D can be delayed without affecting the project schedule. The number of days an activity can be delayed without affecting the overall project schedule is its *float*.

   4b. Late Finish for Activity D is the Late Start for Activity H.

   4c. Late Start for Activity D is found by subtracting the Duration from the Late Finish.
   LS = LF – Duration: 19 – 3 = **16**

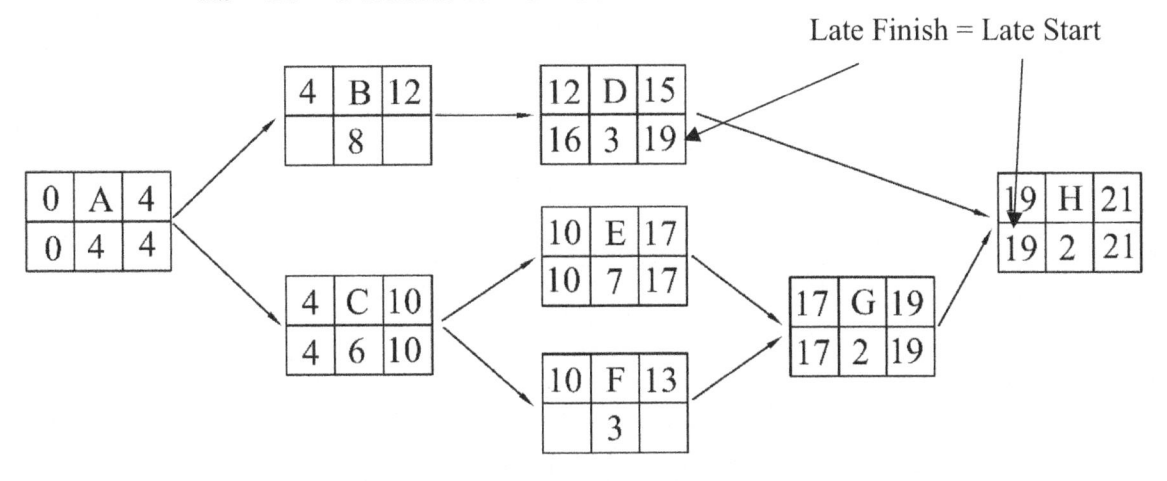

5. Determine float for activity D.

12	D	15
16	3	19

Float = LS − ES = LF - EF **CERM EQ 86.1**

Float = 16 − 12 = 19 − 15 = **4 days**

THE CORRECT ANSWER IS C.

Problem 5 Solution

Which of the following joints is used when concrete has been poured at different times?

A) Contraction Joint
B) Isolation Joint
C) Control Joint
D) Construction Joint

SOLUTION

I. DEFINITIONS

- Contraction Joint – **CERM 77-12** - Used to create a thinner pavement section in one location to encourage shrinkage cracking along that line, usually sawn into pavement
- Isolation Joint – **CERM 77-12** - Used to relieve compressive stresses in the pavement where it adjoins another structure such as bridges or intersections
- Control Joint – **CERM 77-12** - See Contraction Joint
- Construction Joint – **CERM 77-12** - Used transversely between construction periods and longitudinally between pavement lanes

II. GAME PLAN

1. Match term to the correct definition

III. EXECUTE

A *Construction Joint* is used when concrete has been poured at different times.

THE CORRECT ANSWER IS D.

Problem 6 Solution

A 20-foot wall form subjected to a 10 psf wind load is shown in the figure below. Diagonal braces 8-foot on center along the length of the wall prevent the brace from overturning. What is the axial force (lb/ft) resisted by the brace per unit width of wall?

A) 81
B) 202
C) 1143
D) 1616

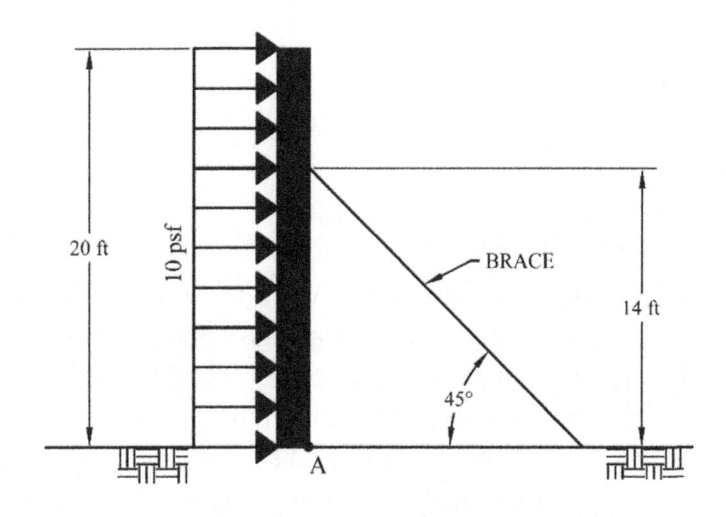

SOLUTION

I. DEFINITIONS

- Axial Force – **CERM 41-12** – The X-component and Y-component of a force acting on a member

II. GAME PLAN

1. Determine the total force applied to the wall from the wind load.
2. Determine the moment about point A.
3. Solve for the axial force, F.
4. Solve for force per unit width of wall.

III. EXECUTE

1. Determine the total force applied to the wall from the wind load.

    Total Force = (wind load)(brace height)(brace spacing)
    Total Force = $\left(10 \frac{lb}{ft^2}\right)(20 \text{ ft})(8 \text{ ft}) =$ **1600 lb**

2. Determine the moment about point A.

    Assume point A acts as a hinge.

    Total force due to wind load = 1600 lb; applied at center of brace.

    Split the force of the brace into its X and Y components.

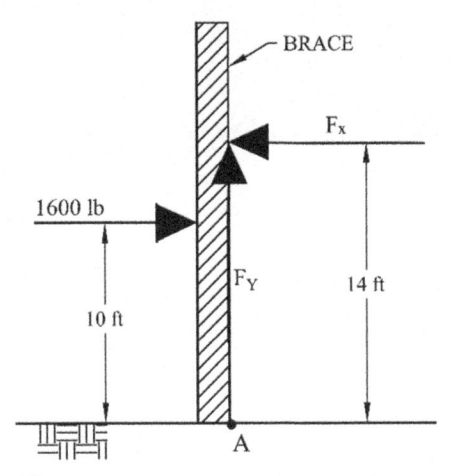

$\sum M_A = 0$, clockwise is positive

$(1600 \text{ lb})(10 \text{ ft}) - (F_X)(14 \text{ ft}) = 0$

$F_X = \frac{(1600 \text{ lb})(10 \text{ ft})}{14 \text{ ft}}$

$F_X = 1143$ lb

3. Solve for the Axial Force, F.

   $\cos 45 = \frac{1143}{F}$

   $F = \frac{1143}{\cos 45}$

   $F = 1616$ lb per brace

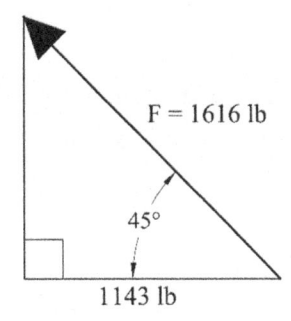

4. Solve for force per unit width of wall.

   Force per unit width of wall $= \frac{\text{force per brace}}{\text{brace spacing}}$

   Force per unit width of wall $= \frac{1616 \text{ lb}}{8 \text{ ft}}$

   Force per unit width of wall $= 202 \frac{\text{lb}}{\text{ft}}$

THE CORRECT ANSWER IS B.

Problem 7 Solution

For the cable system shown, the tension (kips) in cable AB is most nearly:

A) 42.4
B) 44.6
C) 56.5
D) 58.0

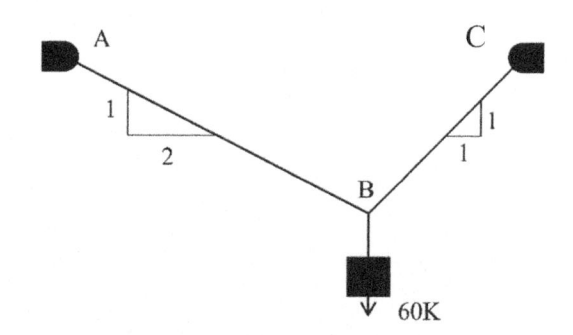

SOLUTION

I. DEFINITIONS

- Ideal Cable – CERM 41-17 – Acts as an axial two-force tension member between points of concentrated loading, assumed to be completely flexible, massless, and incapable of elongation
- Free Body Diagram – CERM 41-9 – A representation of a body in equilibrium, showing all applied forces, moments, and reactions

II. GAME PLAN

1. Draw the free body diagram for Joint B.
2. Sum forces in the X-direction.
3. Sum forces in the Y-direction.
4. Solve for tension in AB.

III. EXECUTE

1. Draw the free body diagram for Joint B.

    Assume all forces are in tension.

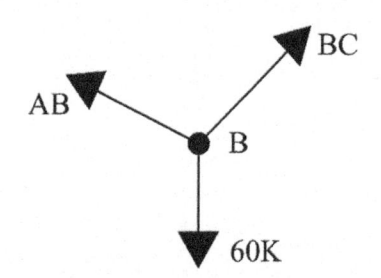

2. Sum forces in the X-direction.

    $\sum F_X = 0$

$F_{AB_X} = F_{BC_X}$

The X-component of $F_{AB} = \frac{2}{2.23}$

The X-component of $F_{BC} = \frac{1}{1.41}$

$AB\left(\frac{2}{2.23}\right) = BC\left(\frac{1}{1.41}\right)$

$0.896 AB = 0.709 BC$

BC = 1.263AB   EQUATION 1

3. Sum forces in the Y-direction.

$\sum F_Y = 0$

$F_{AB_Y} + F_{BC_Y} = 60$

The Y-component of $F_{AB} = \frac{1}{2.23}$

The Y-component of $F_{BC} = \frac{1}{1.41}$

$AB\left(\frac{1}{2.23}\right) + BC\left(\frac{1}{1.41}\right) = 60$

0.448AB + 0.709BC = 60   EQUATION 2

4. Solve for tension in AB.

Using Equations 1 and 2, solve for AB.

   Plug equation 1 into Equation 2.

BC = 1.263AB   EQUATION 1

0.448AB + 0.709BC = 60   EQUATION 2

0.448AB + 0.709(1.263AB) = 60

0.448AB + 0.895AB = 60

1.343AB = 60

AB = 44.67 Kips

THE CORRECT ANSWER IS B.

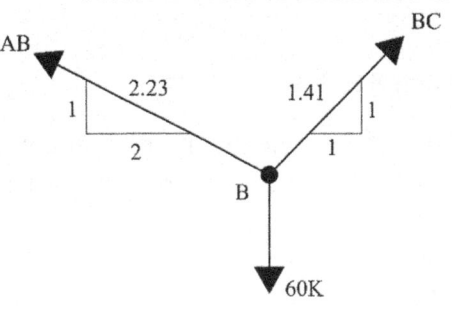

Problem 8 Solution

A 10-ft tall concrete gravity retaining wall having a unit weight of 150 pcf is shown in the figure. The Rankine active earth pressure (lb/ft) is most nearly:

A) 536
B) 2300
C) 2437
D) 2719

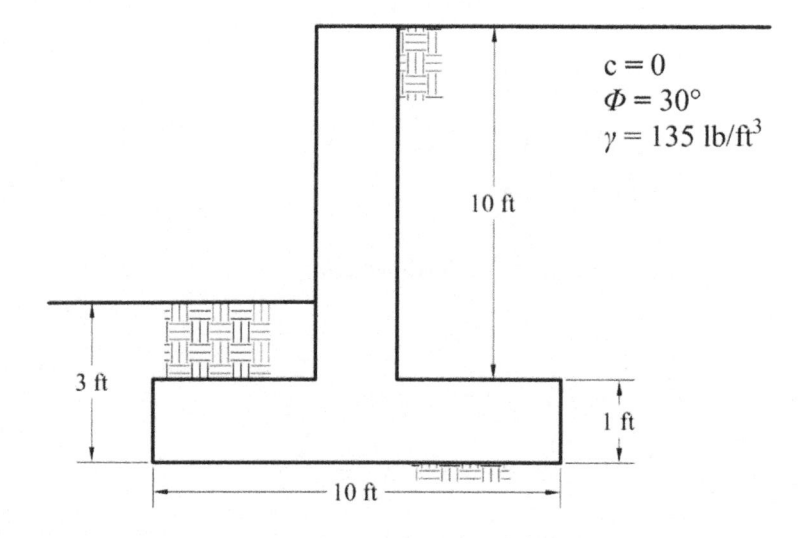

SOLUTION

I. DEFINITIONS

- Earth Pressure – **CERM 37-2** – Force per unit area exerted by soil on the retaining wall
- Active Earth Pressure (R_a) – **CERM 37-2** – Forward soil pressure, present behind a retaining wall that moves away from and tensions the remaining soil
- Rankine Earth Pressure Theory – **CERM 37-2** – Assumes that failure occurs along a flat plane behind the wall inclined at an angle α from the horizontal

II. GAME PLAN

1. Define given terms.
2. Define Rankine Active Earth Pressure Equation.
3. Solve for P_a.
4. Solve for R_a.

III. EXECUTE

1. Define given terms.

    c = cohesion
    β = sloping backfill, degrees
    φ = internal friction angle, degrees
    γ = unit weight of soil, pcf

2. Define Rankine Active Earth Pressure Equation.

$$R_a = \tfrac{1}{2} P_a H \qquad \textbf{CERM EQ 37.10}$$

Civil PE Testing Services

3. Solve for P_a.

$$P_a = K_a P_v - 2c\sqrt{K_a} \qquad \textbf{CERM EQ. 37.4}$$

For granular soils, c = 0 and the equation resolves to:

$$P_a = K_a P_v \qquad \textbf{CERM EQ 37.9}$$

Since the backfill is horizontal and the wall face is vertical, K_a can be defined as:

$$K_a = tan^2(45° - \frac{\varphi}{2}) \qquad \textbf{CERM EQ 37.7}$$

$$K_a = tan^2(45° - \frac{30°}{2})$$

$$\mathbf{K_a = 0.333}$$

Table 37.3 can also be used to determine K_a values

Vertical soil pressure, P_v is defined as:

$$P_v = \gamma H \qquad \textbf{CERM EQ 37.3(b)}$$

Where:

γ = unit weight of soil, pcf

H = wall height measured from heel of retaining wall, ft

$$P_v = \left(135 \frac{lbf}{ft^3}\right)(10 \text{ ft} + 1 \text{ft})$$

$$\mathbf{P_v = 1485 \frac{lbf}{ft^2}}$$

Therefore:

$$P_a = K_a P_v$$

$$P_a = 0.333\left(1485 \frac{lbf}{ft^2}\right)$$

$$\mathbf{P_a = 494.5 \frac{lbf}{ft^2}}$$

4. Solve for R_a.

$$R_a = \frac{1}{2} P_a H \qquad \textbf{CERM EQ. 37.10}$$

$$R_a = \frac{1}{2}(494.5 \frac{lbf}{ft^2})(10 \text{ ft} + 1 \text{ ft})$$

$$\mathbf{R_a = 2719.8 \frac{lbf}{ft}}$$

THE CORRECT ANSWER IS D.

Problem 9 Solution

A 5'x 5' footing is to be constructed near an existing 24" stormsewer. What increase in pressure, in psf, will the center of the pipe experience due to the construction of the footing?

A) 20
B) 34
C) 35
D) 500

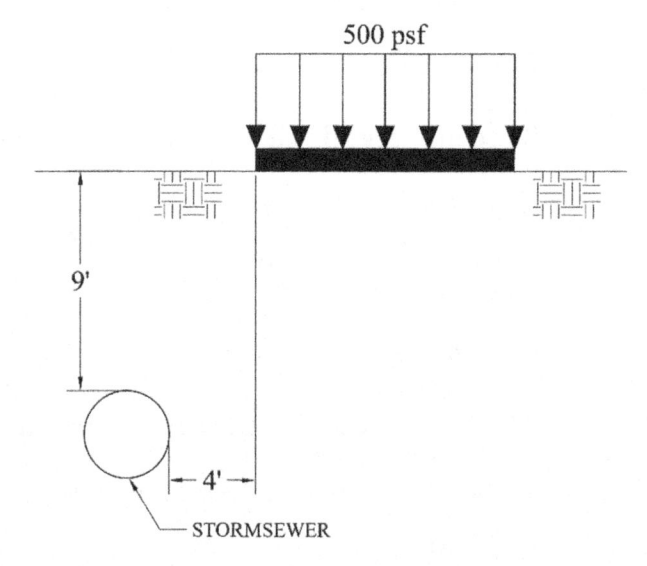

SOLUTION

I. DEFINITIONS

- Footing – **CERM 36-2** – An enlargement at the base of a load-supporting column that is designed to transmit forces to the soil
- Vertical Soil Pressure (Δp_v) – **CERM 37-3** – Pressure caused by the soil's own weight
- Boussinesq's Contour Chart – **CERM 40-2, A-125** – Used to determine the increase in vertical pressure caused by application of a uniformly distributed load
- Boussinesq's Equation – **CERM 40-2** – Used to determine the increase in vertical pressure caused by application of a point load

II. GAME PLAN

1. Define given terms.
2. Use Boussinesq's Contour Chart to determine the load factor.
3. Solve for increase in vertical pressure.

III. EXECUTE

1. Define given terms.

    Footing width, B = 5 ft

    Vertical distance to center of pipe = $9 \text{ ft} + \left(\frac{24 \text{ in}}{2}\right)\left(\frac{1 \text{ ft}}{12 \text{ in}}\right) = 10$ ft or 2B

    Horizontal distance to center of pipe from center of foundation:

    $\frac{5 \text{ ft}}{2} + 4 \text{ ft} + \left(\frac{24 \text{ in}}{2}\right)\left(\frac{1 \text{ ft}}{12 \text{ in}}\right) = 7.5$ ft or 1.5B

2. Use Boussinesq's Contour Chart to determine the load factor.

   - Boussinesq contour chart can be found on **A-125** or **APPENDIX 40.A**
   - Use the chart on the right for a square foundation.
   - Horizontal distance = 1.5B, Vertical distance = 2B
   - **Load factor = 0.04p, from Boussinesq's Stress Contour Chart**
   - Note: because the foundation is uniformly loaded and not a point load, the contour chart is used instead of Boussinesq's equation (CERM EQ. 40.1)

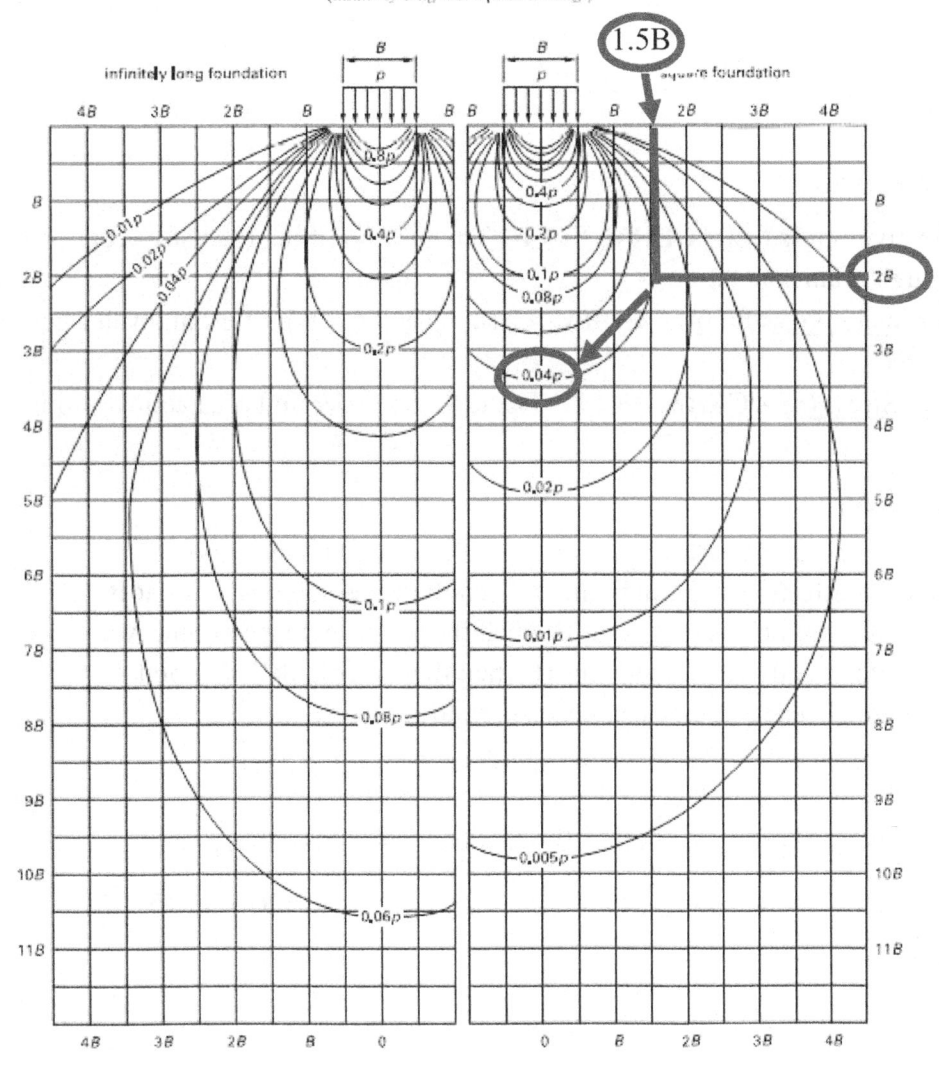

3. Solve for increase in vertical pressure.

   Load factor = 0.04p, p = applied force per square foot or 500 psf

   $$\Delta p_v = 0.04p$$

   $$\Delta p_v = 0.04 \left(500 \frac{\text{lb}}{\text{ft}^2}\right) = 20 \frac{\text{lb}}{\text{ft}^2}$$

THE CORRECT ANSWER IS A.

Problem 10 Solution

Which statement is most true about point B when the water table is raised from point B to point A?

A) The effective stress and pore pressure increase
B) The effective stress and pore pressure decrease
C) The effective stress increases and pore pressure decreases
D) **The effective stress decreases and pore pressure increases**

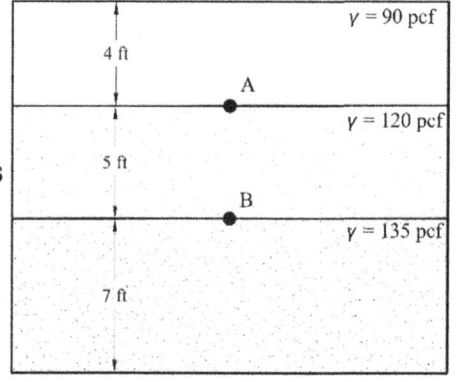

SOLUTION

I. DEFINITIONS

- Effective Stress (σ') – **CERM 35-14** – The portion of the total stress that is supported through grain contact
- Pore Water Pressure (u) – **CERM 35-14** – The pressure of groundwater held within a soil or rock
- Total Stress (σ) – **CERM 35-14** – The total force per unit area acting within a mass of soil

II. GAME PLAN

1. Calculate pore pressure at point B when the water table is at point B.
2. Calculate effective stress at point B when the water table is at point B.
3. Calculate pore pressure at point B when the water table is at point A.
4. Calculate effective stress at point B when the water table is at point A.
5. Compare effective stresses and pore pressures.

III. EXECUTE

1. Calculate pore pressure at point B when the water table is at point B.

$$u = \gamma_w h \qquad \text{CERM 35-15}$$

Where:

u = pore pressure, $\frac{lb}{ft^2}$

γ_w = unit weight of water, $62.4 \frac{lb}{ft^3}$

h = height of water table, ft

$u_B = \left(62.4 \frac{lb}{ft^3}\right)(0 \text{ ft})$

$u_B = 0 \frac{lb}{ft^2}$

2. Calculate effective stress at point B when the water table is at point B.

$\sigma' = \sigma - u$ **CERM EQ 35.17**

Where:

σ' = effective stress, $\frac{lb}{ft^2}$

σ = total stress, $\frac{lb}{ft^2}$

u = pore pressure, $\frac{lb}{ft^2}$

$\sigma = \gamma h$ **CERM 35-15**

Where:

γ = unit weight of soil, $\frac{lb}{ft^3}$

H = height, ft

$\sigma_B = \left(90 \frac{lb}{ft^3}\right)(4 \text{ ft}) + \left(120 \frac{lb}{ft^3}\right)(5 \text{ ft})$

$\sigma_B = 960 \frac{lb}{ft^2}$

Therefore:

$\sigma'_B = \sigma_B - u_B$

$\sigma'_B = 960 \frac{lb}{ft^2} - 0 \frac{lb}{ft^2}$

$\boldsymbol{\sigma'_B = 960 \frac{lb}{ft^2}}$

3. Calculate pore pressure at point B when the water table is at point A.

$u = \gamma_w h$ **CERM 35-15**

$u_A = \left(62.4 \frac{lb}{ft^3}\right)(5 \text{ ft})$

$\boldsymbol{u_A = 312 \frac{lb}{ft^2}}$

4. Calculate effective stress at point B when the water table is at point A.

$\sigma = \gamma h$ **CERM 35-15**

$\sigma_A = \left(90 \frac{lb}{ft^3}\right)(4 \text{ ft}) + \left(120 \frac{lb}{ft^3}\right)(5 \text{ ft})$

$\sigma_A = 960 \frac{lb}{ft^2}$

Therefore:

$$\sigma'_A = \sigma_A - u_A$$

$$\sigma'_A = 960 \frac{lb}{ft^2} - 312 \frac{lb}{ft^2}$$

$$\sigma'_A = 648 \frac{lb}{ft^2}$$

5. Compare effective stresses and pore pressures.

$$\sigma'_B = 960 \frac{lb}{ft^2} \qquad u_B = 0 \frac{lb}{ft^2}$$

$$\sigma'_A = 648 \frac{lb}{ft^2} \qquad u_A = 312 \frac{lb}{ft^2}$$

Pore pressure increases when the water table is raised from point B to point A.

Effective stress decreases when the water table is raised from point B to point A.

THE CORRECT ANSWER IS D.

Problem 11 Solution

A uniformly distributed surface load is applied to the ground surface. The primary consolidation, in inches, for the normally consolidated clay shown below is:

A) 0.9
B) 1.2
C) 1.8
D) 2.6

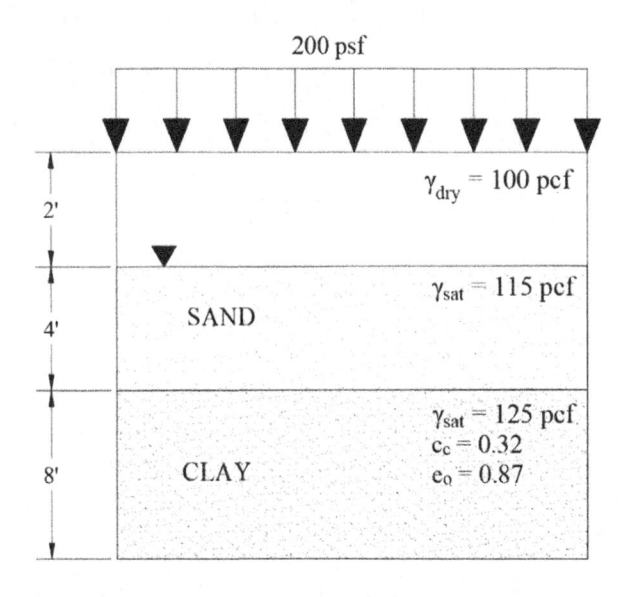

SOLUTION

I. DEFINITIONS

- Primary Consolidation ($S_{primary}$) – **CERM 40-5** – The long-term consolidation due to water loss
- Normally Consolidated Clay – **CERM 40-4** – Virgin clay that has never experienced vertical stress higher than its current condition
- Effective Stress (σ') – **CERM 35-14** – The portion of total stress that is supported through grain contact

II. GAME PLAN

1. Determine primary consolidation equation and define given terms.
2. Determine p_o'.
3. Solve for primary consolidation.

III. EXECUTE

1. Determine primary consolidation equation and define given terms.

$$S_{primary} = \frac{HC_c \log_{10}\frac{p_o' + \Delta p'_v}{p'_o}}{1+e_o} \qquad \textbf{CERM 40.16}$$

Where:

H = thickness of clay layer, feet
C_c = compression index
p'_o = original effective stress at the midpoint of the clay layer and directly below the foundation, psf
p'_v = additional loading, psf

e_o = initial void ratio

2. Determine p'_o.

$$p'_o = \sigma' = H_1 \gamma_{d,sand} + H_2(\gamma_{sat,sand} - \gamma_{water}) + \frac{H_3}{2}(\gamma_{sat,clay} - \gamma_{water})$$

$$p'_o = \sigma' = (2\text{ ft})(100\tfrac{\text{lb}}{\text{ft}^3}) + (4\text{ ft})\left(115\tfrac{\text{lb}}{\text{ft}^3} - 62.4\tfrac{\text{lb}}{\text{ft}^3}\right) + \frac{8\text{ ft}}{2}\left(125\tfrac{\text{lb}}{\text{ft}^3} - 62.4\tfrac{\text{lb}}{\text{ft}^3}\right)$$

$$p'_o = \sigma' = 200\tfrac{\text{lb}}{\text{ft}^2} + 210.4\tfrac{\text{lb}}{\text{ft}^2} + 250.4\tfrac{\text{lb}}{\text{ft}^2}$$

$$\mathbf{p'_o = \sigma' = 660.8\tfrac{\text{lb}}{\text{ft}^2}}$$

3. Solve for primary consolidation.

$$S_{primary} = \frac{HC_c \log_{10}\frac{p'_o + \Delta p'_v}{p'_o}}{1+e_o} \qquad\qquad \textbf{CERM 40.16}$$

$$S_{primary} = \frac{(8\text{ ft})(0.32)\log_{10}\frac{660.8\tfrac{\text{lb}}{\text{ft}^2} + 200\tfrac{\text{lb}}{\text{ft}^2}}{660.8\tfrac{\text{lb}}{\text{ft}^2}}}{1+0.87}$$

$$\mathbf{S_{primary} = 0.15\text{ ft} = 1.8\text{ inches}}$$

THE CORRECT ANSWER IS C.

Problem 12 Solution

An earthen dam is initially dry. If the water table is rapidly raised to the level shown, the dam's factor of safety against slope failure will:

A) Increase
B) Decrease
C) Stay the same
D) Not enough information

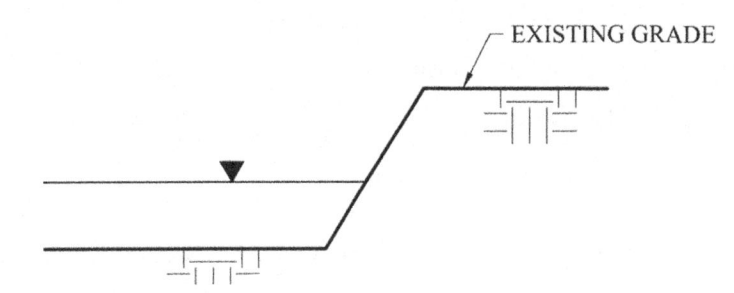

SOLUTION

I. DEFINITIONS

- Cohesive Factor of Safety ($F_{cohesive}$) – **CERM 40-8** – The ratio of resisting force to the sliding or driving force
- Slope Failure – **CERM 40-8** – Rapid or progressive moment of the slope

II. GAME PLAN

1. Determine cohesive factor of safety equation.
2. Determine γ_{eff} at initial condition.
3. Determine γ_{eff} at final condition.
4. Compare γ_{eff} for initial and final conditions.
5. Compare $F_{cohesive}$ for initial and final conditions.

III. EXECUTE

1. Determine cohesive factor of safety equation.

$$F_{cohesive} = \frac{N_o c}{\gamma_{eff} H} \quad\quad \textbf{CERM EQ 40.28}$$

Where:
  N_o = stability number
  c = cohesion, psf
  γ_{eff} = soil unit weight, pcf
  H = depth of the cut, ft

2. Determine γ_{eff} at initial condition.

   At initial condition, the dam is dry. Therefore:

   $\gamma_{eff} = \gamma_{dry}$

3. Determine γ_{eff} at final condition.

   At final condition, the dam is submerged. Therefore:

$$\gamma_{eff} = \gamma_{sat} - \gamma_{water} \qquad \textbf{CERM EQ. 40.29}$$

4. Compare γ_{eff} for initial and final conditions.

    At initial condition, $\gamma_{eff} = \gamma_{dry}$

    At final condition, $\gamma_{eff} = \gamma_{sat} - \gamma_{water}$
    Therefore:

    $$\gamma_{eff_{initial}} > \gamma_{eff_{final}}$$

5. Compare $F_{cohesive}$ for initial and final conditions.

    $$F_{cohesive} = \frac{N_o c}{\gamma_{eff} H} \qquad \textbf{CERM EQ. 40.28}$$

    Since γ_{eff} is in the denominator,

    $$F_{cohesive_{intital}} < F_{cohesive_{final}}$$

    The dam's factor of safety against slope failure will increase.

THE CORRECT ANSWER IS A.

Problem 13 Solution

A 4'x4' square footing is shown below. The factor of safety is 3.0. The maximum net allowable bearing capacity, in psf, is:

A) 11,996
B) 13,559
C) 13,689
D) 15,074

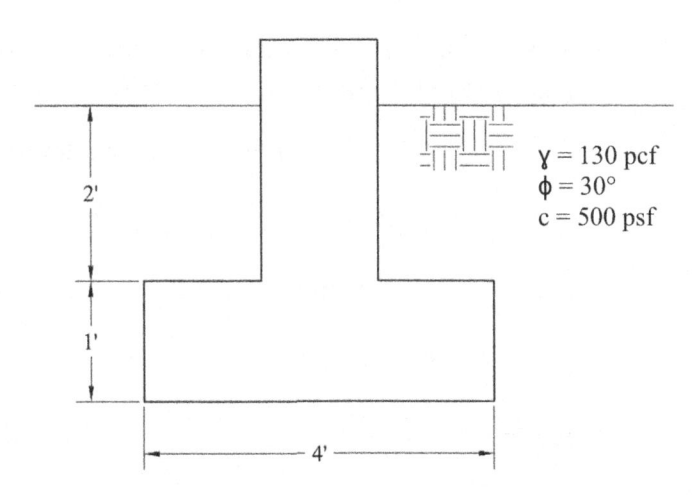

γ = 130 pcf
φ = 30°
c = 500 psf

SOLUTION

I. DEFINITIONS

- Footing – **CERM 36-2** – An enlargement at the base of a load-supporting column that is designed to transmit forces to the soil
- Factor of Safety (FS) – **CERM 36-4** – The ratio of the ultimate strength of a member or a piece of material to the actual working stress or the maximum permissible stress when in use
- Ultimate Bearing Capacity (q_{ult}) – **CERM 36-3** – The theoretical maximum pressure which can be supported without failure
- Net Bearing Capacity (q_{net}) – **CERM 36-4** – The net pressure that can be applied to the footing by an external load that will just initiate failure in the underlying soil
- Net Allowable Bearing Capacity (q_a) – **CERM 36-2** – The net pressure in excess of the overburden stress that will not cause shear failure or excessive settlements

II. GAME PLAN

1. Determine the ultimate bearing capacity.
2. Determine the net bearing capacity.
3. Determine the net allowable bearing capacity.

III. EXECUTE

1. Determine the ultimate bearing capacity.

$$q_{ult} = \tfrac{1}{2}\gamma B N_\gamma + cN_c + \gamma D N_q \qquad \textbf{CERM 36.1(b)}$$

where:

γ = soil unit weight, pcf

B = foundation width, ft

N_γ, N_c, N_q = bearing capacity factors

c = soil cohesion, psf

D = foundation depth, ft

However, a shape factor must be applied for square footings. The shape factors are presented in CERM Table 36.4 and Table 36.5.

Values for N_γ, N_c, N_q can be found via interpolation in CERM Table 36.2.

$q_{ult} = \frac{1}{2}\gamma B N_\gamma(0.85) + (1.25)cN_c + \gamma D N_q$

$q_{ult} = \frac{1}{2}(130\frac{lb}{ft^3})(4\text{ ft})(19.7)(0.85) + (1.25)\left(500\frac{lb}{ft^2}\right)(37.2) + \left(130\frac{lb}{ft^3}\right)(3\text{ ft})(22.5)$

$q_{ult} = 4353.7\frac{lb}{ft^2} + 23250\frac{lb}{ft^2} + 8775\frac{lb}{ft^2}$

$\mathbf{q_{ult} = 36378.7\frac{lb}{ft^2}}$

2. Determine the net bearing capacity.

$q_{net} = q_{ult} - \gamma D$ **CERM 36.7(b)**

$q_{net} = 36378.7\frac{lb}{ft^2} - \left(130\frac{lb}{ft^3}\right)(3\text{ft})$

$\mathbf{q_{net} = 35988.7\frac{lb}{ft^2}}$

3. Determine the net allowable bearing capacity.

$q_a = \frac{q_{net}}{FS}$ **CERM 36.4**

$q_a = \frac{35988.7\frac{lb}{ft^2}}{3.0}$

$\mathbf{q_a = 11996.23\frac{lb}{ft^2}}$

THE CORRECT ANSWER IS A.

Problem 14 Solution

The stress-strain curve for a steel beam is shown below. The maximum tensile strength occurs at which point?

A) Point A
B) Point B
C) Point C
D) Point D

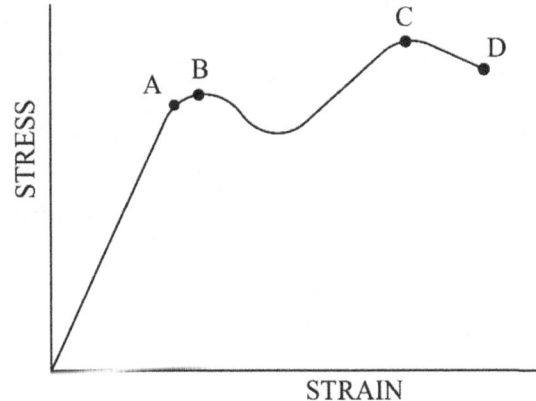

SOLUTION

I. DEFINITIONS

- Elastic Limit – **CERM 43-2** – Applied stress higher than this point results in permanent deformation when the stress is removed
- Yield Point – **CERM 43-3** – Yield strength, the stress that accompanies the beginning of plastic strain
- Ultimate Strength – **CERM 43-3** – Tensile strength, maximum stress the material can support without failure
- Fracture Point – **CERM 43-3** – Breaking strength, stress at which the material actually fails

II. GAME PLAN

1. Reference **CERM Figure 43.3** and match the correct definition.

III. EXECUTE

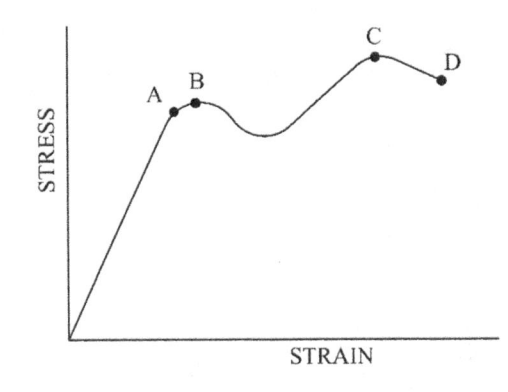

A – Elastic Limit
B – Yield Point
C – Ultimate Strength
D – Fracture Point

1. Referencing **CERM Figure 43.3**, Point C represents the *Ultimate Strength*, also known as *Tensile Strength*

THE CORRECT ANSWER IS C.

Problem 15 Solution

The beam shown below has one pin and one roller connection. The maximum shear force, in kips, in the beam is:

A) 4.2
B) 12.0
C) 13.6
D) 20.0

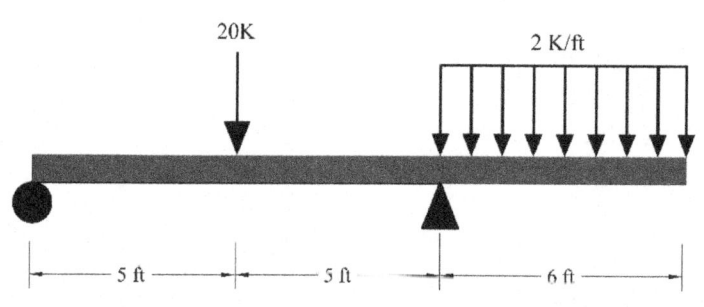

SOLUTION

I. DEFINITIONS

- Shear – **CERM 44-8** – The sum of all vertical forces acting on an object
- Pinned Connection – **CERM 41-7** – Supports both vertical and horizontal forces
- Roller Connection – **CERM 41-7** – Supports vertical forces only
- Shear Diagram – **CERM 44-9** – A graph of shear as a function of position along a beam
- Free Body Diagram – **CERM 41-9** – A representation of a body in equilibrium, showing all applied forces, moments, and reactions

II. GAME PLAN

1. Solve for reactions at supports.
   1a. Set moment about point B equal to zero, determine F_A.
   1b. Sum forces in Y-direction to determine F_B.
2. Draw free body diagram for beam.
3. Draw shear diagram for beam.
4. Determine maximum shear stress in the beam.

III. EXECUTE

1. Solve for reactions at supports.

   1a. Set moment about point B equal to zero, determine F_A.

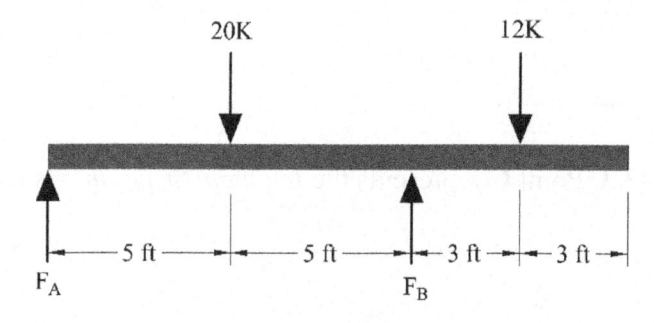

$\sum M_B = 0$, clockwise is positive

$(F_A)(10 \text{ ft}) - (20 \text{ K})(5 \text{ ft}) + (12 \text{ K})(3 \text{ ft}) = 0$

$(F_A)(10 \text{ ft}) = 64 \text{ K} \cdot \text{ft}$

$\mathbf{F_A = 6.4 \text{ K}}$

1b. Sum forces in Y-direction to determine F_B.

$\sum F_Y = 0$

$6.4 \text{ K} - 20 \text{ K} + F_B - 12 \text{ K} = 0$

$\mathbf{F_B = 25.6 \text{ K}}$

2. Draw free body diagram for beam.

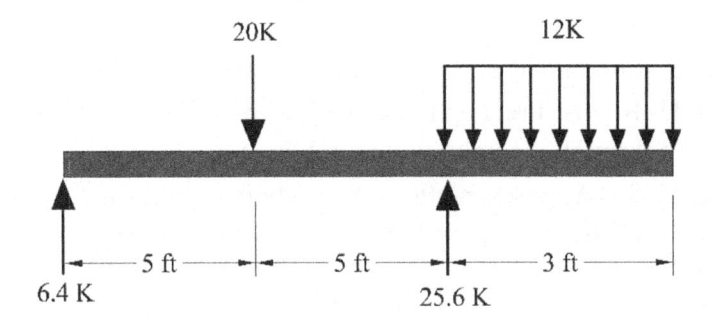

3. Draw shear diagram for beam.

   Start on the left side of the beam and work towards the right.

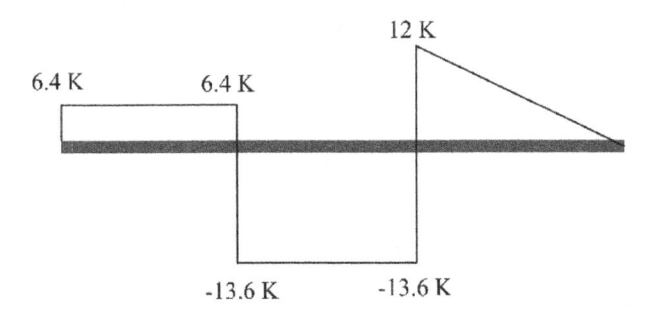

4. Determine maximum shear force in the beam.

   The maximum shear force in the beam is 13.6 Kips.

THE CORRECT ANSWER IS C.

Problem 16 Solution

Analyze the truss shown. The force in member BE, in kips, is most nearly:

A) 1.6
B) 3.7
C) 4.2
D) 5.8

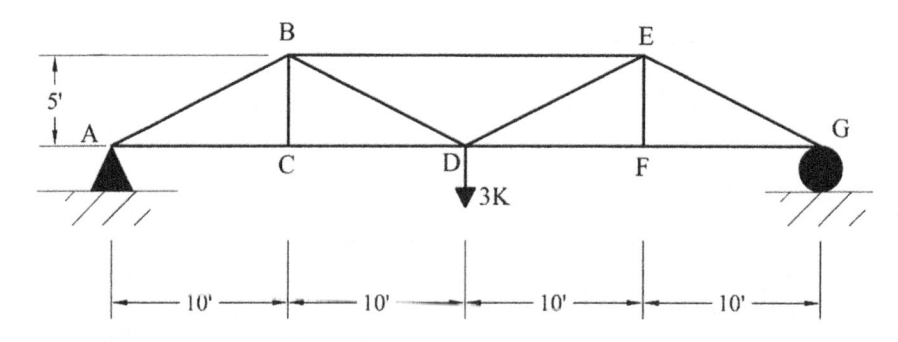

SOLUTION

I. DEFINITIONS

- Truss – **CERM 41-13** – A set of pin-connected axial members connected at joints
- Method of Sections – **CERM 41-16** – A direct approach to finding forces in any truss by cutting through the truss passing through the unknown member
- Free Body Diagram – **CERM 41-9** – A representation of a body in equilibrium, showing all applied forces, moments, and reactions

II. GAME PLAN

1. Determine reactions at supports.
   - **1a.** Set moment about point A equal to zero.
   - **1b.** Sum forces in Y-direction.
2. Cut section through BE and draw free body diagram
   - **2a.** Determine angle θ.
   - **2b.** Sum forces in Y-direction.
   - **2c.** Set moment about A equal to zero.

III. EXECUTE

1. Determine reactions at supports.

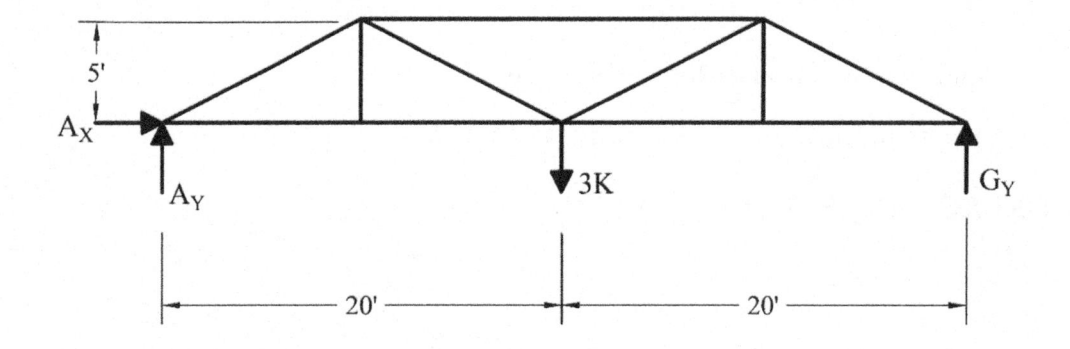

$\sum F_X = 0$

$A_X = 0$

1a. Set moment about point A equal to zero.

$\sum M_A = 0$, clockwise is positive.

$(3\,k)(20\,ft) - (G_y)(40\,ft) = 0$

$G_Y = 1.5\,\text{kips}$

1b. Sum forces in Y-direction.

$\sum F_Y = 0$

$A_Y + G_Y - 3\,k = 0$

$A_Y + 1.5\,k - 3\,k = 0$

$A_Y = 1.5\,\text{kips}$

2. Cut section through BE and draw free body diagram

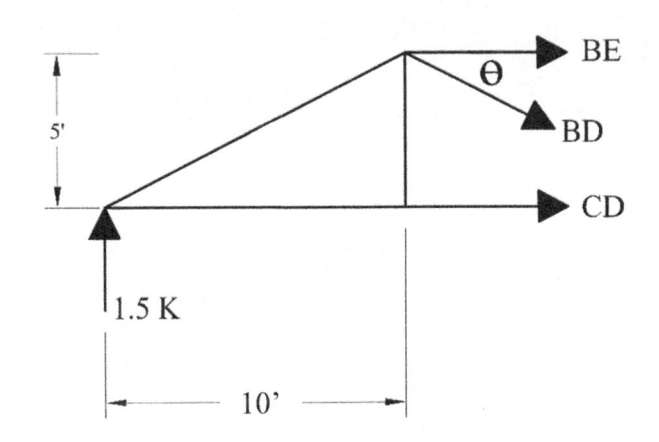

2a. Determine angle θ.

$\tan\theta = \frac{5}{10}$

$\tan^{-1}(0.5) = \theta$

$\theta = 26.5°$

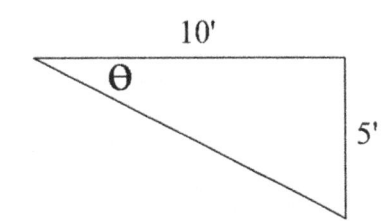

2b. Sum forces in Y-direction.

$\sum F_Y = 0$

$1.5 - BD\sin(26.5) = 0$

$BD = 3.3\,\text{kips}$

2c. Set moment about A equal to zero.

$\sum M_A = 0$, clockwise is positive.

$BE(5 \text{ ft}) + BD\cos(26.5)(5 \text{ ft}) + BD\sin(26.5)(10 \text{ ft}) = 0$

$BE(5 \text{ ft}) + (4.4 \text{ ft})BD + (4.4 \text{ ft})BD = 0$

$BE(5 \text{ ft}) = (-8.88 \text{ ft})BD$

$BE(5 \text{ ft}) = (-8.88 \text{ ft})(3.3 \text{ kips})$

BE = −5.8 kips (compression)

THE CORRECT ANSWER IS D.

Problem 17 Solution

The elongation, in inches, of the 1-foot diameter cylinder due to the applied load is most nearly:

A) 0.000763
B) 0.0000212
C) 0.0000636
D) 0.00000176

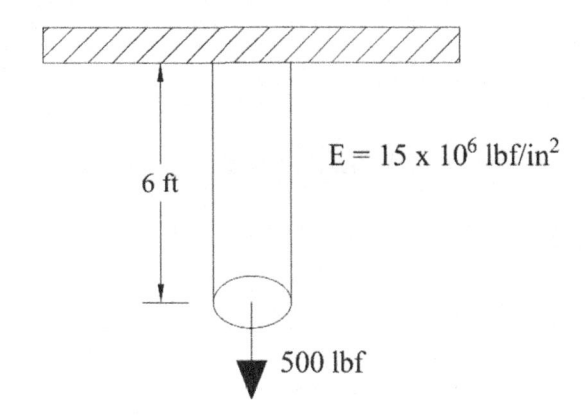

$E = 15 \times 10^6 \text{ lbf/in}^2$

6 ft

500 lbf

SOLUTION

I. DEFINITIONS

- Elongation (δ) – **CERM 43-6** – The amount of extension of an object under stress
- Modulus of Elasticity (E) – **CERM 43-2** – The measures of an object's resistance to deformation when a stress is applied

II. GAME PLAN

1. Determine elastic deformation equation and define given terms.
2. Calculate cylinder area.
3. Solve for elastic deformation.

III. EXECUTE

1. Determine elastic deformation equation and define given terms.

    $$\delta = \frac{L_o F}{EA}$$ **CERM 44.4**

    Where:
    L_o = original length, in
    F = applied force, lbf
    E = Modulus of Elasticity, psi
    A = area normal to force, in^2

2. Calculate cylinder base area.

    $A = \pi r^2$
    $A = \pi (0.5 \text{ ft})^2$
    $A = 0.785 \text{ ft}^2$

    Convert to square inches:
    $A = (0.785 \text{ ft}^2)\left(\frac{144 \text{ in}^2}{1 \text{ ft}^2}\right) = \mathbf{113.1 \text{ in}^2}$

Civil PE Testing Services

3. Solve for elastic deformation.

$$\delta = \frac{L_o F}{EA}$$ **CERM EQ. 44.4**

$$\delta = \frac{(6 \text{ ft})(\frac{12 \text{ in}}{1 \text{ ft}})(500 \text{ lb})}{\left(15 \times 10^6 \frac{\text{lb}}{\text{in}^2}\right)(113.1 \text{ in}^2)}$$

$$\delta = 0.0000212 \text{ inch}$$

THE CORRECT ANSWER IS B.

Problem 18 Solution

The T beam below experiences a bending moment of 1.4 k-ft. The max bending stress in the beam, in psi, is most nearly:

A) 117
B) 125
C) 473
D) 545

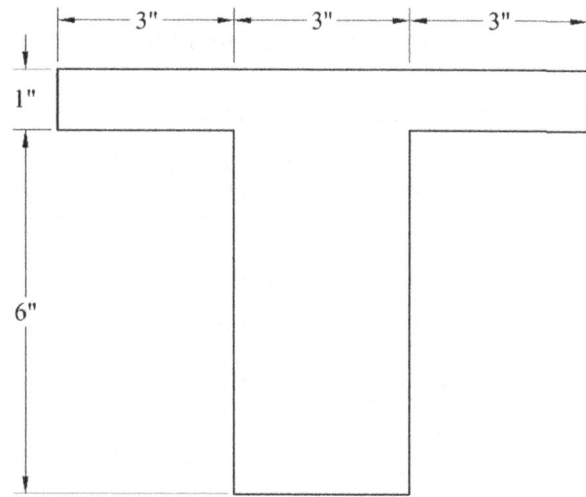

SOLUTION

I. **DEFINITIONS**

- Bending Stress – **CERM 44-11** – Stress in a beam caused by a transverse force, lower surface of the beam experiences tensile stress while the upper surface of the beam experiences compressive stress. There is no stress along a horizontal plane passing through the centroid of the cross section
- Centroid – **CERM 42-1** – The center of gravity of a homogenous body
- Moment of Inertia – **CERM 42-4** – A measure of the beam's ability to resist bending
- Centroidal Moment of Inertia – **CERM 42-4** – The moment of inertia taken with respect to an axis passing through the area's centroid
- Parallel Axis Theorem – **CERM 42-4** – The moment of inertia with respect to another parallel axis

II. **GAME PLAN**

1. Determine bending stress equation and define given terms.
2. Convert bending moment to lb-in.
3. Determine distance, C.
4. Determine moment of inertia about centroid.
5. Solve for bending stress.

III. **EXECUTE**

1. Determine bending stress equation and define given terms.

$$\sigma_{b,max} = \frac{Mc}{I_c}$$ **CERM EQ. 44.37**

Where:

$\sigma_{b,max}$ = maximum bending stress, psi

M = bending moment, lb · in

c = distance from the neutral axis to most distant top or bottom surface, in

I_c = centroidal moment of inertia of the beam's cross section, in⁴

2. Convert bending moment to lb-in.

$$(1.4 \text{ kip} \cdot \text{ft}) \left(\frac{1000 \text{ lb}}{1 \text{ kip}}\right)\left(\frac{12 \text{ in}}{1 \text{ ft}}\right) = \mathbf{16,800 \text{ lb} \cdot \text{in}}$$

3. Determine distance, c.

    3A. Split the T-Beam into two rectangles. Determine Y_c.

$$Y_c = \frac{\sum_i A_i Y_{c,i}}{\sum_i A_i} \qquad \textbf{CERM EQ. 42.6}$$

$$Y_c = \frac{(A_1)(Y_{a1}) + (A_2)(Y_{a2})}{(A_1 + A_2)}$$

$$Y_c = \frac{(9 \text{ in})(1 \text{ in})(6.5 \text{ in}) + (3 \text{ in})(6 \text{ in})(3 \text{ in})}{(9 \text{ in})(1 \text{ in}) + (3 \text{ in})(6 \text{ in})}$$

$$Y_c = c = \mathbf{4.16 \text{ in}}$$

4. Determine moment of inertia about centroid.

$$I_{cx} = \frac{bh^3}{12} \qquad \textbf{CERM APP. 42.A}$$

$$I_{\text{parallel axis}} = I_{cx} + Ad^2 \qquad \textbf{CERM EQ. 42.20}$$

Where:

I_{cx} = moment of inertia about the centroidal axis, in⁴

A = area, in²

d = distance between centroidal axis and parallel axis, in

Area 1:

$$I_1 = \frac{bh^3}{12} + Ad^2$$

$$I_1 = \frac{(9 \text{ in})(1 \text{ in})^3}{12} + (9 \text{ in})(1 \text{ in})(6.5 \text{ in} - 4.16 \text{ in})^2$$

$$I_1 = 50.0 \text{ in}^4$$

Area 2:

$$I_2 = \frac{bh^3}{12} + Ad^2$$

$$I_2 = \frac{(3 \text{ in})(6 \text{ in})^3}{12} + (3 \text{ in})(6 \text{ in})(4.16 \text{ in} - 3 \text{ in})^2$$

$$I_2 = 78.2 \text{ in}^4$$

$$I_c = I_1 + I_2$$

$$I_c = 50.0 \text{ in}^4 + 78.2 \text{ in}^4$$

$$I_c = 128.2 \text{ in}^4$$

5. Solve for bending stress.

$$\sigma_{b,max} = \frac{Mc}{I_c} \qquad \textbf{CERM EQ. 44.37}$$

$$\sigma_{b,max} = \frac{(16{,}800 \text{ lb·in})(4.16 \text{ in})}{128.2 \text{ in}^4}$$

$$\sigma_{b,max} = 545.1 \frac{\text{lb}}{\text{in}^2}$$

THE CORRECT ANSWER IS D.

Problem 19 Solution

The design criteria for all sections in a structural beam are:

A) $\varphi M_n \geq M_u$
B) $\varphi M_n \geq V_u$
C) $V_u \geq \varphi V_n$
D) All the above

SOLUTION

I. DEFINITIONS

- Nominal Value (n) – **CERM 50-4** – Being in accordance with theory for the specified dimensions and material properties
- Strength Reduction Factor (φ) – **CERM 50-4** – Capacity reduction factor, applied to convert the nominal capacity into design capacity, or design strength
- Shear Strength (v) – **CERM 44-8** – The sum of all vertical forces acting on an object
- Moment (M) – **CERM 44-8** – The total bending moment acting on an object

II. GAME PLAN

1. Determine the design criteria for structural beams.

III. EXECUTE

1. The design criteria for all sections in a beam, as given on **CERM 50-4**, are:

   - $\varphi M_n \geq M_u$
   - $\varphi V_n \geq V_u$

THE CORRECT ANSWER IS A.

Problem 20 Solution

The head loss, in feet, through Branch B is most nearly:

A) 4.2
B) 6.8
C) 8.0
D) 14.0

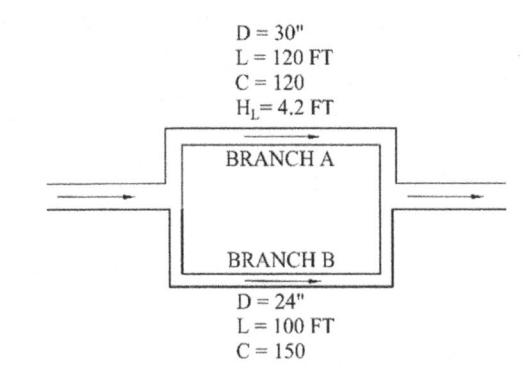

SOLUTION

I. DEFINITIONS

- Pipe Loop – CERM 17-22 – A set of two pipes placed in parallel, both originating and terminating at the same junction
- Head Loss (H_L) – CERM 17-5 – The loss of pressure or "head" that occurs in pipe flow due to friction

II. GAME PLAN

1. Determine the properties of parallel pipe systems.
2. Set the head loss of Branch B equal to the head loss of Branch A.

III. EXECUTE

1. Determine the properties of parallel pipe systems.

    The principals that govern the distribution of flow between the two branches are given on **CERM 17-22**.

    The flow divides in such a manner as to make the head loss in each branch the same.

    Simply stated: the head loss through Branch A is equal to the head loss through Branch B $h_{L,A} = h_{L,B}$

2. Set the head loss of Branch B equal to the head loss of Branch A.

    $h_{L,A} = h_{L,B}$

    The head loss through Branch A is given in the problem, therefore no calculation is necessary.

    $h_{L,A} = 4.2 \text{ feet} = h_{L,B}$

THE CORRECT ANSWER IS A.

Problem 21 Solution

A 48-inch concrete pipe (n = 0.013) flows full during a 100-year rain event. The pipe collects runoff from a 5-acre area. The slope of the pipe is 2%. What is the flow rate, in cfs, under full conditions?

A) 128
B) 204
C) 13,000
D) 154,000

SOLUTION

I. DEFINITIONS

- Mannings Equation – **CERM 19-4** – An empirical equation that applies to uniform flow in open channels
- Mannings Roughness (n) – **CERM 19-4** – The measure of the amount of frictional resistance water experiences while traveling in a channel or pipe
- Hydraulic Radius (R) – **CERM 19-3** – The ratio of the area in flow to the wetted perimeter

II. GAME PLAN

1. Define Manning's Equation.
2. Calculate the Hydraulic Radius.
3. Calculate area of the pipe.
4. Solve Manning's Equation for flow rate.

III. EXECUTE

1. Define Manning's Equation.

$$Q = \frac{1.49}{n} A R^{\frac{2}{3}} \sqrt{S} \qquad \textbf{CERM EQ. 19.13(b)}$$

Where:

Q = flow rate, $\frac{ft^3}{sec}$

R = hydraulic radius, ft

n = mannings roughness

S = channel slope, $\frac{ft}{ft}$

A = flow area, ft^2

2. Calculate the Hydraulic Radius.

The *Hydraulic Radius* for a circular channel flowing full is defined as one-fourth of the hydraulic diameter, therefore:

$$R = \frac{D}{4}$$ **CERM EQ. 19.2**

Where:

  R = hydraulic radius, ft

  D = pipe diameter, ft

D = 48 in = 4 ft

$$R = \frac{4\ ft}{4} = \mathbf{1\ ft}$$

3. Calculate area of the pipe.

   $A = \pi r^2$

   $A = \pi(2\ ft)^2 = 4\pi$

   $\mathbf{A = 12.56\ ft^2}$

4. Solve Manning's Equation for flow rate.

   $$Q = \frac{1.49}{n} A R^{\frac{2}{3}} \sqrt{S}$$ **CERM EQ. 19.13(b)**

   $$Q = \frac{1.49}{0.013}(12.56\ ft^2)(1\ ft)^{\frac{2}{3}}\sqrt{0.02}$$

   $\mathbf{Q = 204\ cfs}$

THE CORRECT ANSWER IS B.

Problem 22 Solution

Rain falls onto three subcatchments as described in the table below. Rainfall intensity is 4.0 inches per hour. The peak runoff, in cfs, for the three watersheds is most nearly:

A) 5.6
B) 8.3
C) 12.0
D) 26.0

Subcatchment	Area (acre)	Lag (min)	C
I	3.2	20	0.65
II	2.0	48	0.70
III	4.2	55	0.72

SOLUTION

I. DEFINITIONS

- Rainfall Intensity – **CERM 20-5** – The amount of precipitation per hour
- Peak Runoff – **CERM 20-15** – The largest flow at an outlet or through a channel
- Rational Method – **CERM 20-15** – Formula for calculating peak runoff applicable to small areas

II. GAME PLAN

1. Calculate peak runoff for Area 1.
2. Calculate peak runoff for Area 2.
3. Calculate peak runoff for Area 3.
4. Determine total peak discharge.

III. EXECUTE

1. Calculate peak runoff for Area 1.

    $Q_1 = CIA$ **CERM EQ 20.36**

    Where:

    Q = peak discharge, cfs
    C = rational coefficient
    I = rainfall intensity, in/hr
    A = drainage area, acres

    $Q_1 = (0.65)(4.0 \frac{in}{hr})(3.2 \text{ acres})$

    $\mathbf{Q_1 = 8.3 \frac{ft^3}{sec}}$

2. Calculate peak runoff for Area 2.

    $Q_2 = (0.70)(4.0 \frac{in}{hr})(2.0 \text{ acres})$

$$Q_2 = 5.6 \frac{ft^3}{sec}$$

3. Calculate peak runoff for Area 3.

$$Q_3 = (0.72)(4.0 \tfrac{in}{hr})(4.2 \text{ acres})$$

$$Q_3 = 12.1 \frac{ft^3}{sec}$$

4. Determine total peak discharge.

$$Q_{peak} = Q_1 + Q_2 + Q_3$$

$$Q_{peak} = 8.3 \frac{ft^3}{sec} + 5.6 \frac{ft^3}{sec} + 12.1 \frac{ft^3}{sec}$$

$$Q_{peak} = 26.0 \frac{ft^3}{sec}$$

THE CORRECT ANSWER IS D.

Problem 23 Solution

The profile of an open channel is shown below. The hydraulic radius of section C, in feet, is most nearly:

A) 2.0
B) 3.6
C) 4.7
D) 6.5

SOLUTION

I. DEFINITIONS

- Open Channel – **CERM 19-2** – A fluid passageway that allows part of the fluid to be exposed to the atmosphere
- Hydraulic Radius (R) – **CERM 19-3** – The ratio of the area in flow to the wetted perimeter
- Wetted Perimeter (W_P) – **CERM 19-3** – The surface of the channel bottom and sides in direct contact with the aqueous body

II. GAME PLAN

1. Determine the Hydraulic Radius equation.
   1a. Determine area in flow of section C.
   1b. Determine wetted perimeter of Section C.
2. Solve for the Hydraulic Radius.

III. EXECUTE

1. Determine the Hydraulic Radius equation.

   $$R = \frac{A}{P}$$ **CERM EQ. 19.2**

   Where:

   R = hydraulic radius, ft

   A = area in flow, ft^2

   P = wetted perimeter, ft

   1a. Determine area in flow of section C.

   The area in flow is defined as the hatched area in the figure.

   $A = (5\,ft + 3\,ft + 5\,ft)(10\,ft)$

   A = 130 ft^2

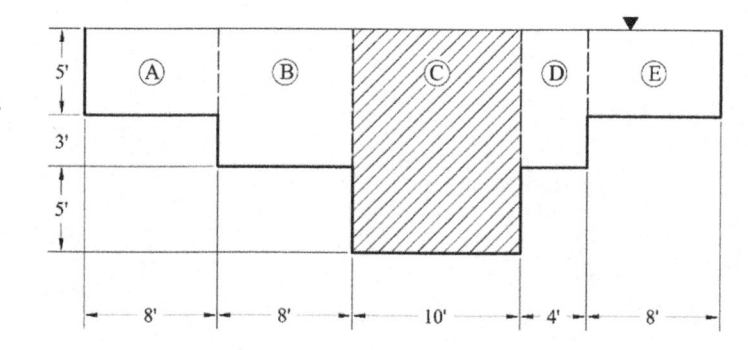

1b. Determine wetted perimeter of Section C.

The wetted perimeter is defined as the bolded line in the figure.

$W_P = (5 \text{ ft} + 10 \text{ ft} + 5 \text{ ft})$

$W_P = 20 \text{ ft}$

2. Solve for the Hydraulic Radius.

$R = \dfrac{A}{P}$

$R = \dfrac{130 \text{ ft}^2}{20 \text{ ft}}$

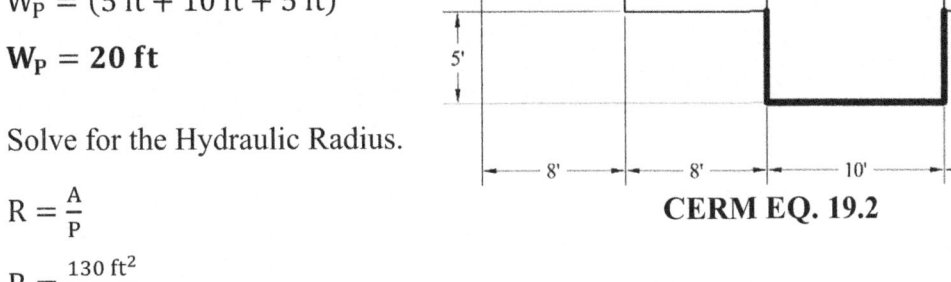

$R = 6.5 \text{ ft}$

CERM EQ. 19.2

THE CORRECT ANSWER IS D.

Problem 24 Solution

Which flow measurement device is used in pressure pipes?

A) Triangular Weir
B) Parshall Flume
C) Orifice Meter
D) Spillway

SOLUTION

I. DEFINITIONS

- Triangular Weir – **CERM 19-13** – V-notch weir, used when small flow rates are to be measured in open channel flow
- Parshall Flume – **CERM 19-15** – Used for measuring open channel wastewater flows, consists of a converging upstream section, a throat, and a diverging downstream section
- Orifice Meter – **CERM 17-32** – Used to measure flow rates in small pipes, consists of a thin or sharp-edged plate with a central, round hole through which the fluid flows
- Spillway – **CERM 19-14** – Used to provide the controlled release of flows from a dam or levee into a downstream area

II. GAME PLAN

1. Match term to correct definition.

III. EXECUTE

An *Orifice Meter* is used to measure flow in pressure pipes.

THE CORRECT ANSWER IS C.

Problem 25 Solution

A 4-hour storm produces a produces a total runoff of 50 acre-ft for a 120-acre watershed. The peak discharge is 650 cfs. The peak discharge for a 4-hour storm producing 3-inches of net precipitation is most nearly:

A) 121
B) 390
C) 650
D) 741

SOLUTION

I. DEFINITIONS

- Unit Hydrograph – **CERM 20-9** – A hydrograph of a storm dropping 1-inch of excess precipitation evenly on the entire watershed

II. GAME PLAN

1. Determine the average precipitation for the watershed.
2. Determine peak discharge for the unit hydrograph.
3. Determine peak discharge for a 3-inch storm.

III. EXECUTE

1. Determine the average precipitation for the watershed.

$$P_{ave} = \frac{V}{A_d} \qquad \textbf{CERM EQ. 20.21}$$

Where:

P_{ave} = average depth of excess precipitation, in
V = runoff volume, acre-ft
A_d = drainage area, acre

$$P_{ave} = \frac{(50 \text{ acre·ft})(\frac{12 \text{ in}}{1 \text{ ft}})}{(120 \text{ acres})}$$

$$\mathbf{P_{ave} = 5 \text{ inch}}$$

2. Determine peak discharge for the unit hydrograph.

$$Q_{p,unit} = \frac{\text{peak discharge}}{P_{ave}}$$

$$Q_{p,unit} = \frac{650 \frac{\text{ft}^3}{\text{sec}}}{5 \text{ in}}$$

$$\mathbf{Q_{p,unit} = 130 \frac{\text{ft}^3}{\text{sec·in}}}$$

3. Determine peak discharge for a 3-inch storm.

$Q_p = (Q_{p,unit})(\text{rainfall depth})$

$Q_p = (130 \frac{ft^3}{sec \cdot in})(3 \text{ in})$

$\mathbf{Q_p = 390 \frac{ft^3}{sec}}$

THE CORRECT ANSWER IS B.

Problem 26 Solution

An 8-inch diameter pipe under 100 psi of pressure discharges through a 2-inch diameter nozzle. Assuming a nozzle coefficient of 1.0, the flow rate through the nozzle, in cfs, is most nearly:

A) 2.65
B) 9.41
C) 42.5
D) 80.2

SOLUTION

I. DEFINITIONS

- Nozzle – CERM 17-34 – A device consisting only of a converging section

II. GAME PLAN

1. Determine nozzle flow equation.
2. Calculate pressure head.
3. Calculate velocity.
4. Calculate flow rate.

III. EXECUTE

1. Determine nozzle flow equation.

    $$V = C_v\sqrt{2gh} \quad\quad\quad \textbf{CERM EQ. 18.60}$$

    Where:

    V = velocity, fps
    C_v = nozzle coefficient
    g = gravity, $32.2 \frac{ft}{sec^2}$
    h = pressure head, ft

2. Calculate pressure head.

    Given pressure = $100 \frac{lb}{in^2}$

    Convert psi to feet of pressure head using the factor 2.308 found in the **CERM Conversion Chart**.

    Pressure head (ft) = $\left(100 \frac{lb}{in^2}\right)(2.308)$
    Pressure head (ft) = **230.8 ft**

3. Calculate velocity.

    $$V = C_v\sqrt{2gh} \quad\quad\quad \textbf{CERM EQ. 18.60}$$

$$V = 1.0\sqrt{2(32.2\tfrac{ft}{sec^2})(230.8\text{ ft})}$$

$$V = 121.9\tfrac{ft}{sec}$$

4. Calculate flow rate.

   Q = VA

   Velocity was found at the nozzle exit, therefore area is also found at the nozzle exit. The nozzle diameter at the exit is 1 inch or 0.083 feet.

   $$Q = \left(121.9\tfrac{ft}{sec}\right)(\pi)(0.083\text{ ft})^2$$

   $$Q = 2.65\tfrac{ft^3}{sec}$$

THE CORRECT ANSWER IS A.

Problem 27 Solution

A 1600-foot-long sag vertical curve joins a tangent of -4% to a tangent of 3%. The BVC is located at stationing 25+00 and elevation 171.00. The elevation and stationing of the lowest point on the curve are most nearly:

	Elevation (ft)	Stationing (ft)
A)	152.7 ft	34+14
B)	152.7 ft	31+85
C)	189.3 ft	34+14
D)	189.3 ft	31+85

SOLUTION

I. **DEFINITIONS**

- Vertical Curve – **CERM 79-12** - A curve used to change the elevations of roadways
- Sag Curve – **CERM 79-12** - A vertical curve that approaches a lower elevation
- BVC - **CERM 79-13** - Beginning of a vertical curve
- G_1 – **CERM 79-13** - Grade from which stationing starts
- G_2 – **CERM 79-13** - Grade towards which stationing heads
- L – **CERM 79-13** - Length of curve
- R – **CERM 79-13** - Rate of change in grade per station
- Turning Point (TP) – **CERM 79-13** - Point on vertical curve where slope is equal to zero, maximum or minimum elevation occurs at this point

II. **GAME PLAN**

1. Draw the sag vertical curve and define given terms.
2. Calculate R.
3. Solve for stationing at the turning point.
4. Solve for elevation at the turning point.

III. **EXECUTE**

1. Draw the sag vertical curve and define given terms.

BVC
STA: 25+00
ELEV: 1710.0
L = 1600'
$G_1 = -4\%$
$G_2 = +3\%$
TURNING POINT

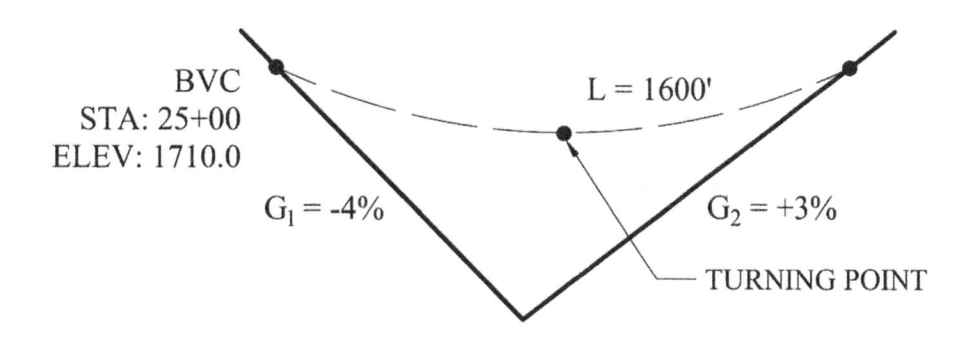

2. Calculate R.

$$R = \frac{G_2 - G_1}{L} \quad \text{CERM EQ 79.46}$$

$$R = \frac{(0.03 - (-0.04))}{1600}$$

R = 0.00004375

3. Solve for stationing at the Turning Point.

$$x_{\text{turning point}} = \frac{-G_1}{R} \quad \text{CERM EQ 79.48}$$

$$x_{\text{turning point}} = \frac{-0.04}{0.00004375}$$

$x_{\text{turning point}} = 914.28$ feet

Stationing of Turning Point = [Sta BVC]+[$X_{\text{turning point}}$]
Stationing of Turning Point = [25+00]+[9+14.28]
Stationing of Turning Point = 34+14.28

4. Solve for elevation at the Turning Point.

$$\text{elev}_x = \frac{Rx^2}{2} + G_1 x + \text{elev}_{BVC} \quad \text{CERM EQ 79.47}$$

$$\text{elev}_{TP} = \frac{(0.00004375)(914.28)^2}{2} + (-0.04)(914.28) + 171.00$$

$\text{elev}_{TP} = 152.71$ feet

THE CORRECT ANSWER IS A.

Problem 28 Solution

A circular horizontal curve with length of 2000 feet is shown below. The middle ordinate, measured in feet, is most nearly:

A) 145
B) 150
C) 155
D) 160

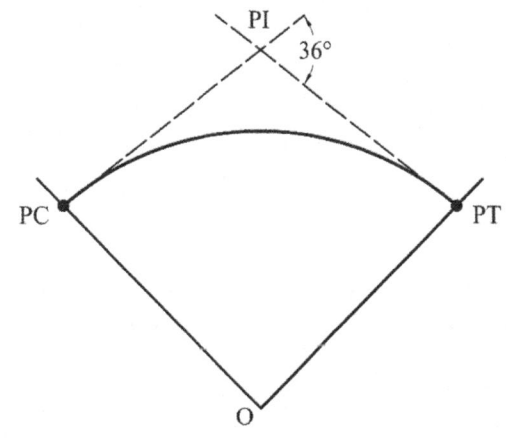

SOLUTION

I. DEFINITIONS

- Horizontal Curve – **CERM 79-2** – A circular arc between two straight lines known as tangents
- Middle Ordinate (M) – **CERM 79-2** – The distance from the midpoint of the curve to the long chord
- Length of Curve (L) – **CERM 79-2** – The length of curve from the PC to the PT
- Point of Curvature (PC) – **CERM 79-2** – The point where the back tangent ends and the curve begins
- Point of Tangency (PT) – **CERM 79-2** – The point where the curve ends and the forward tangent begins
- Point of Intersection (PI) – **CERM 79-2** – The point of intersection of the back and forward tangents
- Intersection Angle (I) – **CERM 79-2** – Central angle of curve; deflection angle between back and forward tangents; interior angle

II. GAME PLAN

1. Draw the horizontal curve and define the givens terms.
2. Calculate the radius of the curve.
3. Calculate the middle ordinate.

III. EXECUTE

1. Draw the horizontal curve and define the givens terms.

Civil PE Practice Exam and Guide

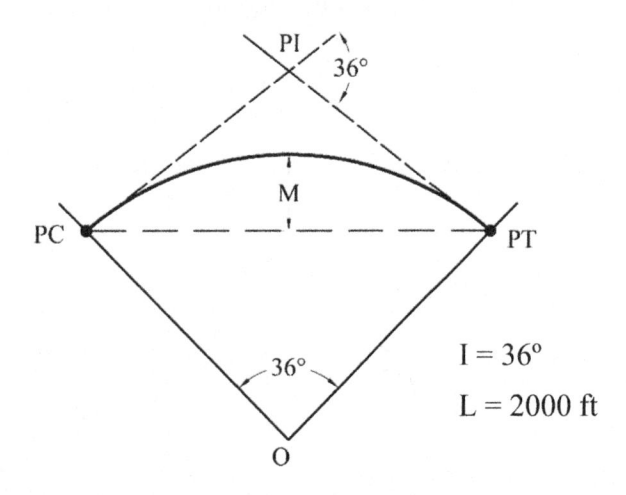

[Diagram of horizontal curve with PI at top (36°), PC on left, PT on right, M in middle, O at bottom with 36° angle, I = 36°, L = 2000 ft]

2. Calculate the radius of the curve.

$$L = \frac{2\pi RI}{360°}$$ **CERM EQ 79.3**

Solving for R:

$$R = \frac{360°L}{2\pi I}$$

Where:

R = radius of curve, ft

L = length of curve, ft

I = interior angle, degree°

$$R = \frac{360°(2000 \text{ ft})}{2\pi(36°)}$$

R = 3183 ft

3. Calculate the middle ordinate.

$$M = R(1 - \cos\frac{I}{2})$$ **CERM EQ 79.6**

$$M = 3183(1 - \cos\frac{36°}{2})$$

M = 155.7 feet

THE CORRECT ANSWER IS C.

Civil PE Testing Services

Problem 29 Solution

Given the following information, determine the annual number of buses in the design lane for a two-lane highway.

AADT = 6000	LOS = C
Peak Factor = 2.0	% Cars = 50%
FFS = 60 mph	% Trucks = 30%
No. lanes each direction = 1	% Buses = 20%
Directional Design = 60/40	

A) 480
B) 720
C) 262,800
D) 438,000

SOLUTION

I. DEFINITIONS

- Average Annual Daily Traffic (AADT) – **CERM 73-5** – The total volume of vehicle traffic on a highway or road for a year divided by 365 days
- Peak Hour Factor (PHF) – **CERM 73-6** – The ratio of the total actual hourly volume to the peak rate of flow within the hour
- Free Flow Speed (FFS) – **CERM 73-7** – The maximum speed for which the density does not affect travel speed
- Level of Service (LOS) – **CERM 73-3** – A user's quality of service through or over a specific facility
- Directional Distribution Factor – **CERM 76-18** – Used to account for the differences in loading according to travel direction

II. GAME PLAN

1. Determine the annual traffic on the two-lane highway.
2. Determine the annual traffic in the design lane.
3. Determine the number of buses in the design lane.

III. EXECUTE

1. Determine the annual traffic on the two-lane highway.

   Annual traffic = (AADT)(365)

   Annual traffic = (6000)(365)

   Annual traffic = 2,190,000 vehicles

2. Determine the annual traffic in the design lane.

   The design lane is the lane with 60% of the traffic therefore:

   Annual traffic in design lane = (Annual Traffic)(60%)

   Annual traffic in design lane = (2,190,000)(60%)

   Annual traffic in design lane = 1,314,000 vehicles

3. Determine the number of buses in the design lane.

   Buses account for 20% of total traffic therefore:

   Annual buses in design lane = (Annual Traffic in design lane)(20%)

   Annual buses in design lane = (1,314,000)(20%)

   Annual buses in design lane = 262,800 buses

THE CORRECT ANSWER IS C.

Problem 30 Solution

What is the best way to compact clean gravel?

A) **Vibratory Roller Compactor**
B) Pneumatic Rubber Tire Roller
C) Sheepsfoot Roller Compactor
D) Smooth-wheel Roller

SOLUTION

I. DEFINITIONS

- Compaction – **CERM G-5** – Densification of soil by mechanical means, involving the expulsion of excess air
- Vibratory Roller Compactor – **CERM 76-9** – Densifies soils via vibration; well suited for cohesionless soils
- Pneumatic Rubber Tire Roller – **CERM 76-9** – Provide a kneading action in the finish roll, used with chip-seal and other thin-surface treatments
- Sheepsfoot Roller Compactor – **CERM 35-18** – Used for cohesive soils, provides a kneading action
- Smooth-wheel Roller – **CERM 35-18** – Used for final finishes and other thin-surface treatments

II. GAME PLAN

1. Match correct definition.

III. EXECUTE

A *Vibratory Roller Compactor* is the best way to compact clean gravel.

THE CORRECT ANSWER IS A.

Problem 31 Solution

The strength over time graph for Portland Cement Type I is shown below. The strength over time graph for Portland Cement Type III is most nearly:

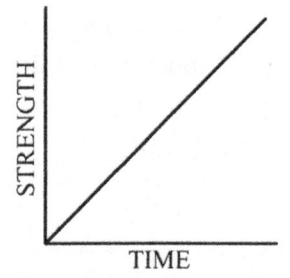

Portland Cement Type I

A)

B)

C)

D)

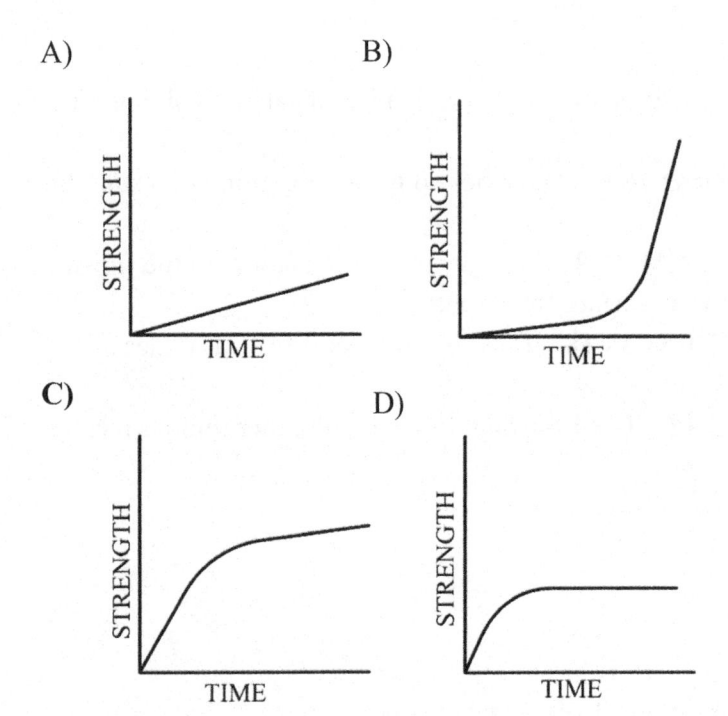

SOLUTION

I. DEFINITIONS

- Portland Cement – **CERM 48-1** – Produced by burning a mixture of lime and clay in a rotary kiln and grinding the resulting mass, used in concrete structures
- Type I Cement – **CERM 48-1** – Normal portland cement: general purpose cement used whenever sulfate hazards are absent and when the heat of hydration will not produce a significant rise in the temperature of the cement
- Type III Cement – **CERM 48-2** – High-early strength portland cement: develops its strength quickly. Suitable for use when a structure must be put into early use or when long-term protection against cold temperatures is not feasible. The ultimate strength is slightly lower than that of type I cement.

II. GAME PLAN

1. Match correct graph with portland cement type III.

III. EXECUTE

1. Match correct graph with portland cement type III.

    The given curve for portland cement type I appears to be at a 1:1 slope. Based on the definition of portland cement type III, type III gains strength quicker than type I. This eliminates graphs A and B.

    Although portland cement type III's ultimate strength is less than that of type I, graph D's ultimate strength is too weak and does not continue to increase over time. Therefore, graph C is correct.

THE CORRECT ANSWER IS C.

Problem 32 Solution

A soil is under investigation. Mechanical and Plasticity limits are shown below. According to the Unified Soil Classification System (USCS), the soil may be classified as:

Mechanical Analysis		Plasticity	
Sieve	% Finer	Liquid Limit	Plastic Limit
10	85%	62	26
40	70%		
200	61%		

A) Fat Clay
B) Lean Clay
C) MH
D) LH

SOLUTION

I. DEFINITIONS

- Unified Soil Classification System (USCS) – **CERM 35-4** – A soil classification system based on grain size distribution, liquid limit, and plasticity index of the soil; soils are classified by a group symbol and a corresponding ground name
- Plasticity – **CERM 35-4** – The property of a soil to be deformed without breaking under external force
- Atterberg Limits – **CERM 35-4** – A basic measure of the critical water contents of a fine-grained soil
- Plastic Limit (PL) – **CERM 35-22** – The water content corresponding to the transition between the semi-solid and plastic state
- Liquid Limit (LL) – **CERM 35-22** – The water content corresponding to the transition between the plastic and liquid state
- Plasticity Index (PI) – **CERM 35-22** – Indicates the range in moisture content over which the soil is in a plastic condition

II. GAME PLAN

1. Use the USCS Classification Table to classify the soil.
   - **1a.** Determine % passing sieve 200; F_{200}.
   - **1b.** Determine Liquid Limit.
2. Classify soil based on Plasticity Chart.
   - **2a.** Determine Plasticity Index.
   - **2b.** Plot soil properties on Plasticity Chart.

III. EXECUTE

1. Use the USCS Classification Table to classify the soil.

Civil PE Practice Exam and Guide

See USCS Chart on next page OR CERM Table 35.5

1a. Determine % passing sieve 200; F_{200}.

The first step in USCS Classification is to determine if the soil is Coarse-Grained or Fine-Grained. This is determined by the percent of material smaller or finer than the No. 200 sieve, F_{200}.

$F_{200} = 61\%$, given in the Mechanical Analysis table

$F_{200} > 50\%$, therefore the soil is Fine-Grained and classification starts at the bottom half of the classification table.

1b. Determine Liquid Limit.

The second step is to determine if the soil has high or low plasticity. This is determined by the Liquid Limit, LL.

LL = 62, given in the Mechanical Analysis table

LL > 50, therefore the soil is highly plastic and classification continues onto the Plasticity Chart.

2. Classify soil based on Plasticity Chart.

   2a. Determine Plasticity Index.

   PI = LL − PL   **CERM EQ 35.23**
   PI = 62 - 26
   PI = 36

   2b. Plot soil properties on Plasticity Chart.

   The Plasticity Chart requires the Plasticity Index (PI) and the Liquid Limit (LL) to classify the soil.

   PI = 36, LL = 62

The soil plots above the A-line on the Plasticity Chart and is highly plastic.

The soil classification is CH, or a Fat Clay.

THE CORRECT ANSWER IS A.

CALIFORNIA DEPARTMENT OF TRANSPORTATION (CALTRANS)

UNIFIED SOIL CLASSIFICATION SYSTEM

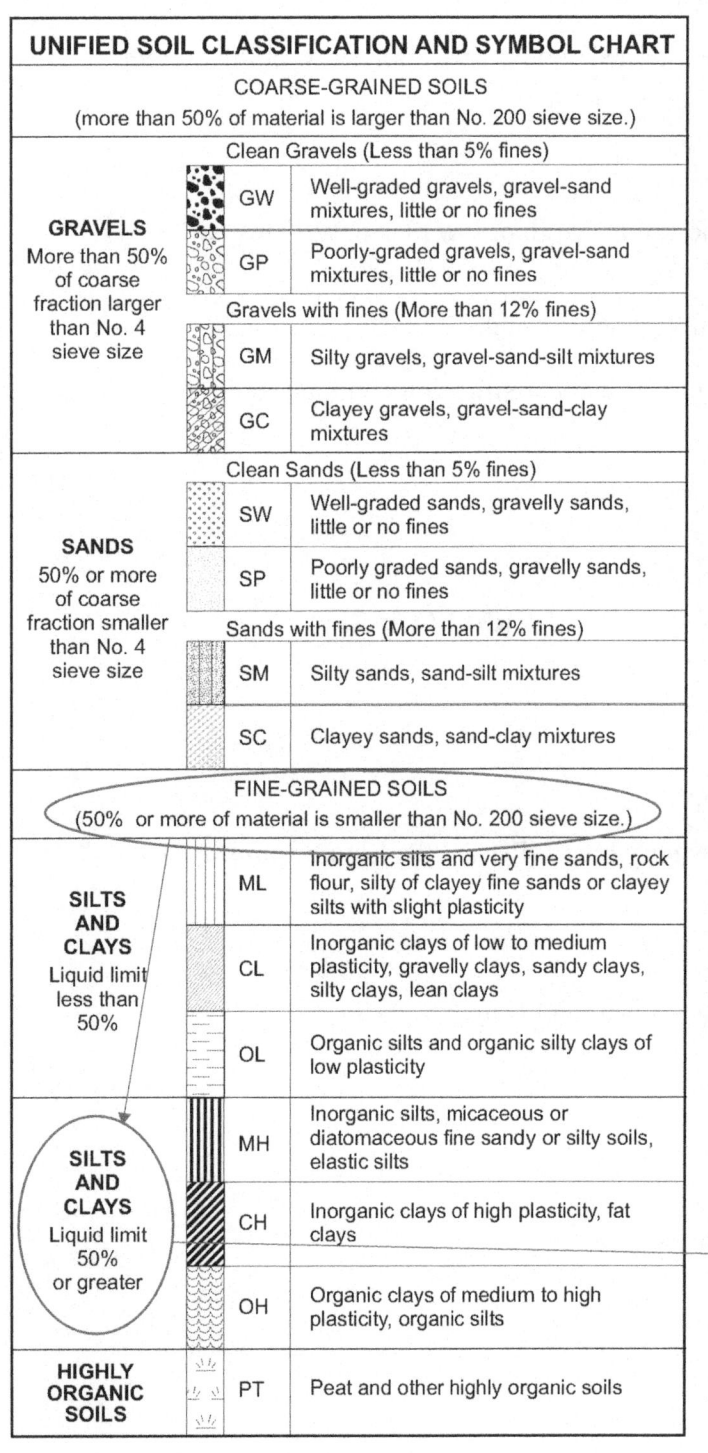

UNIFIED SOIL CLASSIFICATION AND SYMBOL CHART

COARSE-GRAINED SOILS
(more than 50% of material is larger than No. 200 sieve size.)

GRAVELS More than 50% of coarse fraction larger than No. 4 sieve size	Clean Gravels (Less than 5% fines)	GW	Well-graded gravels, gravel-sand mixtures, little or no fines
		GP	Poorly-graded gravels, gravel-sand mixtures, little or no fines
	Gravels with fines (More than 12% fines)	GM	Silty gravels, gravel-sand-silt mixtures
		GC	Clayey gravels, gravel-sand-clay mixtures
SANDS 50% or more of coarse fraction smaller than No. 4 sieve size	Clean Sands (Less than 5% fines)	SW	Well-graded sands, gravelly sands, little or no fines
		SP	Poorly graded sands, gravelly sands, little or no fines
	Sands with fines (More than 12% fines)	SM	Silty sands, sand-silt mixtures
		SC	Clayey sands, sand-clay mixtures

FINE-GRAINED SOILS
(50% or more of material is smaller than No. 200 sieve size.)

SILTS AND CLAYS Liquid limit less than 50%	ML	Inorganic silts and very fine sands, rock flour, silty of clayey fine sands or clayey silts with slight plasticity
	CL	Inorganic clays of low to medium plasticity, gravelly clays, sandy clays, silty clays, lean clays
	OL	Organic silts and organic silty clays of low plasticity
SILTS AND CLAYS Liquid limit 50% or greater	MH	Inorganic silts, micaceous or diatomaceous fine sandy or silty soils, elastic silts
	CH	Inorganic clays of high plasticity, fat clays
	OH	Organic clays of medium to high plasticity, organic silts
HIGHLY ORGANIC SOILS	PT	Peat and other highly organic soils

LABORATORY CLASSIFICATION CRITERIA

GW	$C_u = \dfrac{D_{60}}{D_{10}}$ greater than 4; $C_c = \dfrac{D_{30}}{D_{10} \times D_{60}}$ between 1 and 3
GP	Not meeting all gradation requirements for GW
GM	Atterberg limits below "A" line or P.I. less than 4
GC	Atterberg limits above "A" line with P.I. greater than 7

Above "A" line with P.I. between 4 and 7 are borderline cases requiring use of dual symbols

SW	$C_u = \dfrac{D_{60}}{D_{10}}$ greater than 4; $C_c = \dfrac{D_{30}}{D_{10} \times D_{60}}$ between 1 and 3
SP	Not meeting all gradation requirements for GW
SM	Atterberg limits below "A" line or P.I. less than 4
SC	Atterberg limits above "A" line with P.I. greater than 7

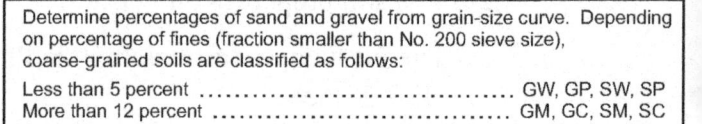

Limits plotting in shaded zone with P.I. between 4 and 7 are borderline cases requiring use of dual symbols.

Determine percentages of sand and gravel from grain-size curve. Depending on percentage of fines (fraction smaller than No. 200 sieve size), coarse-grained soils are classified as follows:

Less than 5 percent .... GW, GP, SW, SP
More than 12 percent .... GM, GC, SM, SC
5 to 12 percent .... Borderline cases requiring dual symbols

PLASTICITY CHART

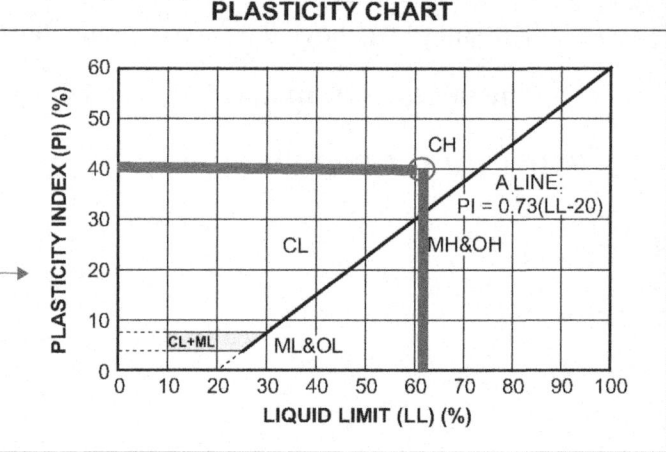

A LINE: PI = 0.73(LL-20)

Zones: CL+ML, ML&OL, CL, CH, MH&OH

Axes: PLASTICITY INDEX (PI) (%) 0–60; LIQUID LIMIT (LL) (%) 0–100

Problem 33 Solution

A soil sample has a specific gravity of 2.65. What is the dry unit weight (lb/ft³) if the soil's water content is 16% and degree of saturation is 73%?

A) 105
B) 107
C) 111
D) 112

SOLUTION

I. DEFINITIONS

- Dry Unit Weight (γ_d) – **CERM 35-8** – The weight of soil solids per unit of total volume of soil mass
- Density (ρ) – **CERM 35-8** – The ratio of the total mass to the total volume
- Specific Gravity (SG) – **CERM 35-8** – A dimensionless ratio of a fluid's density to the density of pure water
- Water Content (ω) – **CERM 35-7** – The ratio of mass of water to the mass of solids
- Degree of Saturation (S) – **CERM 35-7** – The percentage of the volume of water to the total volume of voids

II. GAME PLAN

1. Define given soil properties.
2. Determine equation in CERM Table 35.7 that solves for γ_d using the given properties.
3. Solve for γ_d.

III. EXECUTE

1. Define given soil properties.

    SG = 2.65
    ω = 0.16
    S = 0.73

2. Determine equation in **CERM Table 35.7** that solves for γ_d using the given properties.

$$\gamma_d = \frac{SG(\gamma_w)}{[1+\frac{\omega(SG)}{S}]} \qquad \textbf{CERM Table 35.7}$$

Where:

γ_d = dry unit weight, pcf

SG = specific gravity

γ_w = unit weight of water, pcf

S = degree of saturation, %

ω = water content, %

3. Solve for γ_d.

$$\gamma_d = \frac{SG(\gamma_w)}{[1+\frac{\omega(SG)}{S}]}$$

CERM Table 35.7

$$\gamma_d = \frac{2.65\left(62.4\frac{lbf}{ft^3}\right)}{[1+\frac{0.16(2.65)}{0.73}]}$$

$$\boldsymbol{\gamma_d = 104.6\ \frac{lbf}{ft^3}}$$

THE CORRECT ANSWER IS A.

Civil PE Practice Exam and Guide

Problem 34 Solution

A new construction project requires 200,000 cubic feet of fill. The soil used for fill is to be excavated and hauled from a nearby borrow pit. The borrow soil has a shrinkage factor of 14% and a swell factor of 11%. The required soil volume in cubic yards to be hauled from the borrow pit is most nearly:

A) 9,490
B) 9,560
C) 256,200
D) 258,140

SOLUTION

I. DEFINITIONS

- Borrow Pit – **CERM 80-4** – An area where material has been dug for use at another location
- Shrinkage – **CERM 80-2** – The decrease in volume of earth from its natural state to its compacted state
- Swell – **CERM 80-1** – The change in volume of earth from its natural to loose state
- Bank Cubic Yards (BCY) – **CERM 80-1** – The volume of earth in its natural state
- Loose Cubic Yards (LCY) – **CERM 80-1** – The volume of earth during transport
- Compacted Cubic Yards (CCY) – **CERM 80-1** – The volume of earth after compaction

II. GAME PLAN

1. Determine CCY.
2. Convert CCY to BCY.
3. Convert BCY to LCY.

III. EXECUTE

1. Determine CCY.

    Total fill is given = 200,000 ft³

    $$CCY = (200{,}000 \text{ ft}^3)\left(\frac{1 \text{ yd}^3}{27 \text{ ft}^3}\right) = \mathbf{7407 \text{ yd}^3}$$

2. Convert CCY to BCY.

    $$BCY = \frac{CCY}{1-\text{shrink}}$$ **CERM Table 80.1**

    $$BCY = \frac{7407 \text{ yd}^3}{1-0.14}$$

    $$\mathbf{BCY = 8613 \text{ yd}^3}$$

3. Convert BCY to LCY.

LCY = BCY(1 + swell) **CERM Table 80.1**
LCY = 8613(1 + 0.11)
LCY = 9560 yd³

THE CORRECT ANSWER IS B.

Problem 35 Solution

The results of 28-day concrete cylinder breaks are shown below. The concrete molds are 4" x 8". The 28-day compressive strength, in psi, is most nearly:

A) 10
B) 2437
C) 2666
D) 9753

Cylinder No.	Failure Loading (Kips)
1	130
2	128
3	114
4	118

SOLUTION

I. DEFINITIONS

- Compressive Strength (f'_c) – **CERM 48-4** – The maximum stress a concrete specimen can sustain in compressive axial loading

II. GAME PLAN

1. Calculate average loading at failure.
2. Calculate area of cylinder.
3. Solve for compressive strength.

III. EXECUTE

1. Calculate average loading at failure.

    Average Loading $= \frac{130+128+114+118}{4}$ kips

    Average Loading $= 122.5$ kips $= 122,500$ lbs

2. Calculate area of cylinder.

    $A = \pi r^2$

    $A = \pi (2 \text{ in})^2$

    $A = 12.56 \text{ in}^2$

3. Solve for compressive strength.

    $f'_c = \frac{P}{A}$ **CERM EQ 48.1**

    Where:

    f'_c = compressive strength, psi

    P = maximum axial load, lb

    A = cross sectional area of cylinder, in^2

$$f'_c = \frac{122{,}500 \text{ lbs}}{12.56 \text{ in}^2}$$

$$f'_c = 9753 \ \frac{\text{lb}}{\text{in}^2}$$

THE CORRECT ANSWER IS D.

Problem 36 Solution

The side of a hill is to be excavated for construction of a new 60 ft x 60 ft building. The length of excavation will be 200 ft. How many cubic yards of material will need to be excavated?

A) 1,335
B) 4,445
C) 36,000
D) 120,000

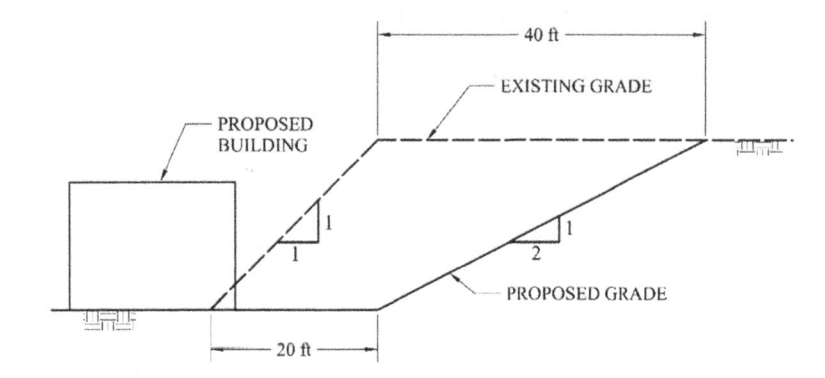

SOLUTION

I. DEFINITIONS

- Excavation – CERM 39-1 - The removal of soil to allow for construction of foundations and other permanent features below the finished level of grade

II. GAME PLAN

1. Calculate area of excavation.
2. Multiply area of excavation by length of excavation.
3. Convert to cubic yards.

III. EXECUTE

1. Calculate area of excavation.

   Area 1 = $(20 \text{ ft})(20 \text{ ft})\left(\frac{1}{2}\right)$

   Area 1 = 200 ft²

   Area 2 = $(20 \text{ ft})(40 \text{ ft})\left(\frac{1}{2}\right)$

   Area 2 = 400 ft²

   Total Area = 200 ft² + 400 ft²

   Total Excavation Area = 600 ft²

2. Multiply area of excavation by length of excavation.

   The length of excavation is given as 200 ft.

   Total Volume of Excavation = (Total Excavation Area)(Length of Excavation)

   Total Volume of Excavation = (600 ft²)(200 ft)

   Total Volume of Excavation = 120,000 ft³

3. Convert to cubic yards.

$$(120{,}000 \text{ ft}^3)\left(\frac{1 \text{ yd}^3}{27 \text{ ft}^3}\right) = 4444 \text{ yd}^3$$

Total Excavation = 4444 yd³

THE CORRECT ANSWER IS B.

Problem 37 Solution

Two wells exist at points A and B. A new well is to be constructed at point C. The coordinates of the points are shown in the figure below. The bearing of line AC is most nearly:

A) N31°E
B) N59°E
C) N31°W
D) S59°W

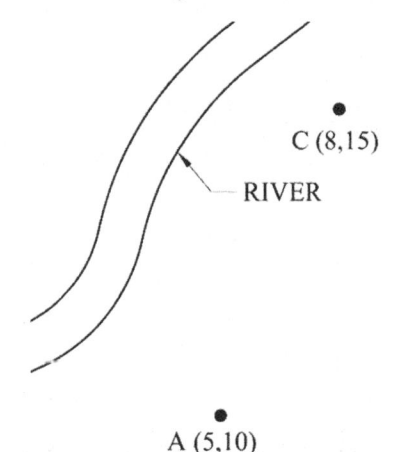

SOLUTION

I. **DEFINITIONS**

- Bearing – CERM 78-13 – A reference to the quadrant in which the line falls and the angle that the line makes with the meridian in that quadrant
- Meridian – CERM 78-12 – An arbitrarily chosen reference line

II. **GAME PLAN**

1. Draw the bearing triangle for line AC
2. Determine bearing triangle side lengths.
3. Determine angle A.
4. Determine bearing of line AC.

III. **EXECUTE**

1. Draw the bearing triangle for line AC.

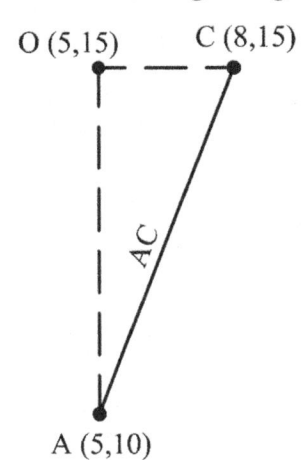

2. Determine bearing triangle side lengths.

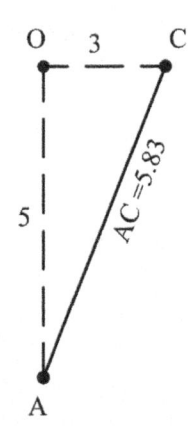

3. Determine angle A.

   Tangent $\theta = \frac{\text{opposite}}{\text{adjacent}}$

   Tan A $= \left(\frac{3}{5}\right)$

   A $= \text{Tan}^{-1}(0.6)$

   A $= 31°$

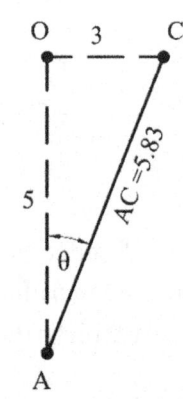

4. Determine bearing of line AC.

   With Point A as the origin, line AC moves north and then 31° east. Therefore:

   Bearing AC $=$ N31°E

THE CORRECT ANSWER IS A.

Problem 38 Solution

The erosion and sediment control feature best used to reduce runoff flow rate is:

A) Silt Fence
B) Sediment Structure
C) Erosion Control Fabric
D) Check Dam

SOLUTION

I. DEFINITIONS

- Silt Fence – **CERM 80-12** – A temporary measure utilizing woven wire or other material attached to posts with filter cloth composed of burlap, plastic filter fabric, and so on to retain the suspended silt particles in the runoff water
- Sediment Structure – **CERM 80-11** – An energy-dissipating rock dump, basin, pond, and trap that catches and stores sediment from upstream erodible areas in order to protect properties and stream channels, including culverts and pipe structures, below the construction site from excessive siltation
- Erosion Control Fabric – **CERM 80-12** – Used on steep slopes to prevent erosion of soil and mulch
- Check Dam – **CERM 80-11** – A barrier composed of logs and poles, large stones, or other material places across a natural or constructed drainway to retard stream flow and catch small sediment loads.

II. GAME PLAN

1. Match the correct definition.

III. EXECUTE

A *Check Dam* is best used to reduce runoff flow rate.

THE CORRECT ANSWER IS D.

Problem 39 Solution

The profile and mass diagrams for a construction project are shown below. Which statement is true?

A) Section B-C represents a fill operation
B) The job transitions from cut to fill at station C
C) The net cut/fill is zero
D) B and C

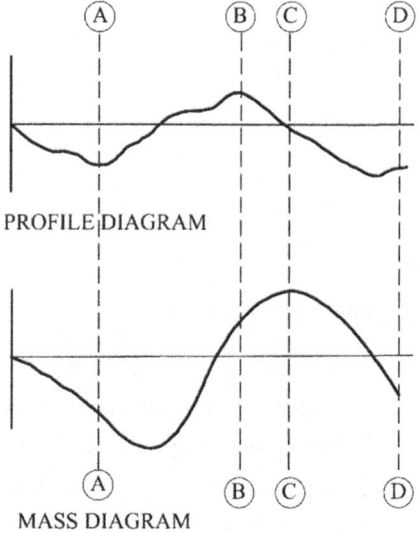

SOLUTION

I. DEFINITIONS

- Profile Diagram – **CERM 80-7** – A cross section of the existing ground elevation along a route alignment
- Mass Diagram – **CERM 80-7** – A record of the cumulative earthwork volume moved along an alignment

II. GAME PLAN

1. Determine action for section B-C.
2. Determine transition at station C.
3. Determine net cut/fill.

III. EXECUTE

1. Determine action for section B-C.

    The X-axis in a profile diagram represents existing grade. A curve above the X-axis represents a cut operation and a curve below the axis represents a fill operation.

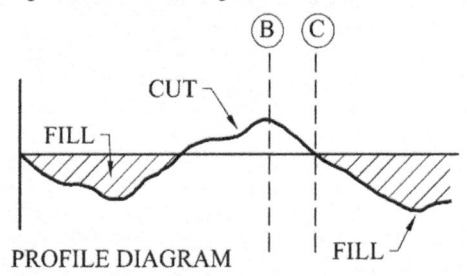

    Station B-C represents a cut operation. **Answer A is false.**

2. Determine transition at station C.

   The point on a profile diagram where a curve crosses the X-axis is known as a *transition point*. For the given profile diagram, the curve slopes from above the X-axis to below it, crossing the axis at station C.

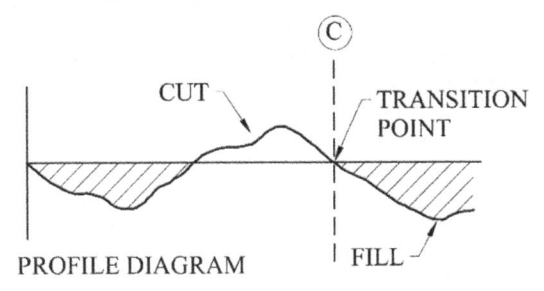

   Station C represents a transition from cut to fill. **Answer B is true.**

3. Determine net cut/fill.

   The net cut/fill can be determined by where the curve ends on the profile diagram. If the curve ends at the X-axis then net cut/fill is zero and the job is balanced. For the profile diagram shown, the curve at station D is below the X-axis. Therefore, there will be net fill and the job is not balanced.

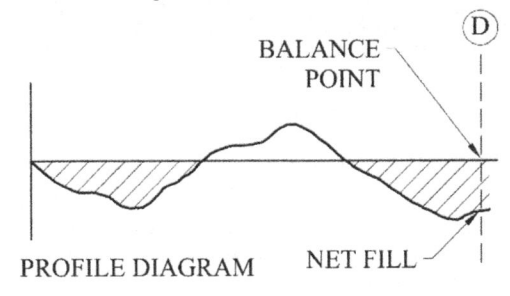

   Answer C is false.

THE CORRECT ANSWER IS B.

Problem 40 Solution

OSHA requires that fall protection be provided for each employee walking or working on an elevated surface. This regulation applies to elevated surfaces, measured in feet, that exceed a height of:

A) 4
B) 6
C) 10
D) 12

SOLUTION

I. DEFINITIONS

- OSHA – **CERM 83-1** - Occupational Safety and Health Administration, regulates workers' safety in the United States
- Fall Protection – **CERM 83-7** – Barricades, walkways, bridges with guardrails, nets and fall arrest systems used for the purpose of preventing falls from elevated surfaces
- OSHA 1926.502(d)(16)(iii) – Personal fall arrest systems, when stopping a fall, shall be rigged such that an employee can neither free fall more than 6 feet nor contact any lower level.

II. GAME PLAN

1. Match the correct OSHA regulation.

III. EXECUTE

1. *OSHA 1926.502(d)(16)(iii)* requires fall protection to be used for elevated surfaces that exceed a height of 6 feet.

THE CORRECT ANSWER IS B.

Made in the USA
Las Vegas, NV
28 March 2024